EZRA POUND

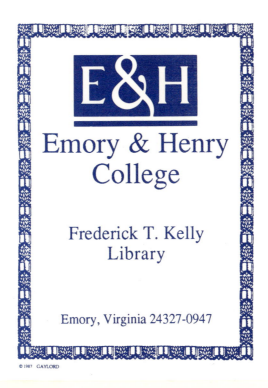

EZRA POUND

The Prime Minister of Poetry

Burton Raffel

ARCHON BOOKS
1984

The paper in this book meets the guidelines for permanence and durability of the Committee on Production Guidelines for Book Longevity of the Council on Library Resources.

Library of Congress Cataloging in Publication Data

Raffel, Burton.
  Ezra Pound, the prime minister of poetry.
  Bibliography: p.
  Includes index.
  1. Pound, Ezra, 1885-1972—Criticism and
interpretation. I. Title.
PS3531.082Z7914   1984   811'.52   84-20533
ISBN 0-208-02061-6

Acknowledgment is made to the following for permission to reprint material:

To New Directions Publishing Corporation for material from:

The Collected Early Poems of Ezra Pound. Copyright © 1976 by the Trustees of the
    Ezra Pound Literary Property Trust. All rights reserved.
Personae. Copyright © 1926 by Ezra Pound.
Translations. Copyright © 1926, 1954, 1957, 1958, 1960, 1962, 1963 by Ezra
    Pound.
The Cantos of Ezra Pound. Copyright © 1934, 1937, 1940, 1948, 1956, 1959, 1962,
    1963, 1965, 1968, 1970 by Ezra Pound.
The Literary Essays of Ezra Pound. Copyright 1935 by Ezra Pound.
Selected Letters. Copyright 1950 by Ezra Pound.
Selected Prose, 1909-1965. Copyright © 1973 by the Estate of Ezra Pound.
Gaudier-Brzeska. Copyright © 1970 by Ezra Pound. All rights reserved.
The Spirit of Romance. Copyright © 1968 by Ezra Pound. All rights reserved.
The ABC of Reading. Copyright © 1934 by Ezra Pound.
Pavannes and Divigations. Copyright © 1958 by Ezra Pound.

To Princeton University Press for an excerpt from Wai-lim Yip, *Ezra Pound's "Cathay."* Copyright © 1969 by Princeton University Press.

To North Point Press for an excerpt from "To Praise the Music," excerpted from: *Life Supports: New and Collected Poems* (c) 1981 by William Bronk. Published by North Point Press and reprinted by permission. All rights reserved.

Contents

Chronology

1885	Ezra Loomis Pound is born in Hailey, Idaho, on October 10
1887	Family moves to New York
1889	Family moves to Philadelphia
1891–1901	Attends private schools in the Philadelphia area
1898	Makes his first trip to Europe, with a great-aunt
1901–1903	Attends the University of Pennsylvania, meets William Carlos Williams
1903–1905	Transfers to Hamilton College, completes B.A. degree
1905–1906	Attends the University of Pennsylvania as a graduate student, studying Spanish, Old French, Provencal, Italian, and Latin literatures; meets Hilda Doolittle (H.D.), to whom he is unofficially engaged; completes M.A. degree
1906	Made Harrison Fellow in Romanics; travels to Europe for the summer
1907	Further graduate work at the University of Pennsylvania; first criticism published; plans but does not write Ph.D. dissertation on Lope de Vega; meets and is engaged to Mary S. Moore of Trenton, New Jersey; takes teaching post in department of French, Spanish, and Italian at Wabash College, Crawfordsville, Indiana

	Sextus Propertius are published; leaves London for Paris
1921	Translates Remy de Gourmont's *Physique de l'Amour*, as *The Natural Philosophy of Love*; *Poems 1918–21* is published; reads, critiques, and helps Eliot to revise *The Waste Land*
1922	*The Natural Philosophy of Love* is published; translates a French adventure novel, Edouard Estaunié's *L'Appel de la route (The Call of the Road)*; meets Ernest Hemingway; Eliot's *The Waste Land* is published
1923	Meets composer George Antheil
1924	Moves to Rapallo, Italy; daughter, Maria, and son, Omar, are born
1925	*A Draft of XVI Cantos* is published; Pound's opera, "Le Testament," is performed
1926	*Personae* is published
1927	Receives *The Dial* Award
1928	*Selected Poems*, edited by Eliot, is published by Faber and Faber; parents moved to Rapallo
1930	*A Draft of XXX Cantos* is published
1931	*How to Read* is published
1932	*Guido Cavalcanti Rime* is published
1933	Has private interview with Mussolini; *ABC of Economics* is published
1934	*ABC of Reading* is published; *Make It New* is published; meets James Laughlin
1935	*Jefferson and/or Mussolini* is published
1936	Lectures on Vivaldi
1937	*Polite Essays* and *The Fifth Decad of Cantos* are published
1938	Becomes member of National Institute of Arts and Letters; *Guide to Kulchur* is published
1939	Visits United States; receives honorary doctorate from Hamilton College
1940	*Cantos LII-LXXI* is published
1941	Translates Enrico Pea's *Moscardino*; begins to broadcast over Radio Rome

1942–1943	Continues to broadcast over Radio Rome
1945	Arrested, confined at Pisa, flown to Washington, charged with treason, and remanded to St. Elizabeth's Hospital
1948	*The Pisan Cantos* is published
1950	*The Lettersof Ezra Pound* is published
1953	*The Translations of Ezra Pound* is published
1954	*Literary Essays of Ezra Pound* is published; *The Classic Anthology Defined by Confucius* is published
1955	*Rock-Drill De Los Cantares* is published
1958	Released from St. Elizabeth's, returns to Italy
1959	*Thrones de los Cantares* is published
1965	Visits England for Eliot's funeral
1969	Visits the United States
1972	Dies on November 1

Preface

Gaul may well have been neatly divisible, but Ezra Pound is not. Much of his poetry is in his translations, and much of his translations is in his poetry; his literary criticism shades over into everything from autobiography to social commentary and discussion of economics, music, art, and whatever else happens to have been passing through his quicksilver but frequently highly disorderly mind. Like Proteus, he is always changing shape; like some mythical literary monster he is always growing here, just when you think you have him pinned down there.

I have not tried to write as Pound wrote. His close friend and longtime associate, Ford Madox Ford, told him as early as 1920 that "Your heart is golden: so are yr words. But the latter are normally—even when they can be read—incomprehensible." I have tried to make rational divisions, so that his life's work might be the more readily displayed and understood. But I have not tried to force Pound into those divisions, nor would it have worked if I had tried. There is more biography in chapter one, here, than in other chapters, but there is biography in all the chapters. There is a chapter devoted primarily to translations, but translations are considered elsewhere as well. The final chapter is devoted to Pound's influence and importance, but that is a subject that must constantly be dealt with, and is here dealt with in every chapter.

I have sought to engage with Pound, as directly as possible, and without the mediation of the vast body of critical literature that had begun to grow around him and his work long before he died. Other critics are mentioned, but not extensively discussed: if I disagree with anyone, I want that disagreement to be with Pound, for he is the subject of this book, and I care very deeply that his work be given respectful and yet critical examination. I have been reading Ezra Pound for almost forty years; I hope that long period of sustained and sometimes passionate attention is reflected in the pages that follow.

1 Introduction

Ezra Pound usually thought of himself as a poet. But as D. H. Lawrence wrote in 1909, after meeting him in London, "his god is beauty," and beauty assumed many forms for Pound. Lawrence distinguished his own concern from Pound's, adding that, as for gods, "mine [is] life."[1] Pound had no doubt "that life has its own satisfactions"; he insisted however that "the satisfactions of art . . . are different from the satisfactions of life." Indeed, "the satisfactions of art differ from the satisfactions of life as the satisfactions of seeing differ from the satisfactions of hearing." And, Pound concluded, "there is no need to dispense with either." On the other hand, "the result of the attempt to mix the satisfactions of art and life is, naturally, muddle."[2]

He pursued beauty all his long life. "It was Ezra who really introduced me to William Morris," wrote the poet H.D., recalling the year 1905. "He literally shouted 'The Gilliflower of Gold' in the orchard."[3] But as the editor of his letters aptly says, "To him art was not something one could practice a certain number of hours a day, with Saturdays and Sundays 'off'. Art was . . . a kind of life."[4] Pound wrote in a myriad of genres and forms: novels (which he burned), drama (which was unperformed), short stories (some of which he published as "pavannes"), translations and adaptations, criticism, journalism, historical and economic commentary, and, of course, poetry in virtually all its genres and forms. But he wrote music, too, including an opera built around texts from the late medieval poet Francois Villon.[5] He took painting lessons, he tried his hand at fencing (he seems to have fenced well), tennis ("to play against him is

1

like playing against an inebriated kangaroo," wrote Ford Madox Ford),[6] even boxing (his teacher was Ernest Hemingway). All his life he took delight in working with his hands, making furniture, repairing it. So too he constructed literary movements, and repaired (and in some cases established) the careers of other artists.

Though he did very little formal teaching, Pound constantly reached out to almost anyone who would listen, explaining, exhorting, correcting. As early as 1916 Carl Sandburg, some seven years Pound's senior, began an essay in *Poetry* magazine with the declaration that "If I were driven to name one individual who, in the English language . . . has done most of living men to incite new impulses in poetry, the chances are I would name Ezra Pound."[7] Sandburg was writing from the United States, and he had felt Pound's influence largely through printed work. T. S. Eliot, writing from London in 1964, said flatly that "Mr. Pound is more responsible for the XXth Century revolution in poetry than is any other individual"—and Eliot was introducing a volume of Pound's literary essays, all designed to aid and instruct those willing to be helped.[8] "Never, in the literary world," said F. R. Leavis after World War Two, "has there been a more courageous single-mindedness. . . . With a patent absence of concern for anything but the reputation, livelihood and development of poets and writers, [he] did what he could to get them published and known, and to make such organs as he could start, commandeer or get a hand in, serve his magnanimous purposes."[9] It was in truth a matter of something very like religion for Pound: assistance to and instruction of other writers, especially younger writers, was for him a moral quest, a charge laid upon him by forces larger and more important than any single human being, himself included. "If a nation's literature declines," wrote Pound, "the nation atrophies and decays. . . . It doesn't matter whether the good writer wants to be useful, or whether the bad writer wants to do harm."[10] Even more drastically, he claims that "Italy went to rot, destroyed by rhetoric, destroyed by the periodic sentence and by the flowing paragraph, as the Roman Empire had been destroyed before her. For when words cease to cling close to things, kingdoms fall, empires wane and diminish."[11]

It was both a personal and an impersonal crusade. In his brief 1972 foreword to a collection of his prose, Pound noted that "the volume would be more presentable had it been possible to remove 80% of the sentences beginning with the pronoun 'I' "[12] Nor did he back only writers he himself liked. "[D. H.] Lawrence, as you know," he told Harriet Monroe in 1913, "gives me no particular pleasure. . . . [But] I *recognize* certain qualities of his work. If I were an editor I should probably accept his work without reading it. As a prose writer I grant him first place among the younger men."[13] The passion with which Pound approached all writing is legendary. In 1917, writing to an editor about typographical errors in galley proofs that had been sent him, he exploded,

> What the ensanguined 11111111111111111111 is the matter with this BLOODY goddman blasted bastardbitchborn-sonofaputridseahorse of a foetid and stinkerous printer ??????. . . JHEEZUSMARIA JOSE!!! Madre de dios y de dios del perro. Sacrobosco di Satanas.[14]

There were many who found his dedication, his energy, and his intensity both personal and annoying. "He had deliberately chosen the path of hostility. Edmund Gosse found him unspeakable."[15] "The Americans, young literary men," wrote the father of the poet, W. B. Yeats, to his son, "found him surly, supercilious and grumpy."[16] The young H.D., half in love with him, recognized that at about age twenty Pound was already "immensely sophisticated, immensely superior, immensely rough-and-ready."[17] "Pound is a fine fellow," wrote the young William Carlos Williams, "but not one person in a thousand likes him, and a great many people detest him and why? Because he is so darned full of conceits and affectation. He is really a brilliant talker and thinker but delights in making himself just exactly what he is not: a laughing boor."[18] Admitting that "his aim [in London] was less to promote Ezra Pound than to propagate new standards for verse," Stanley Weintraub adds that Pound "had large ambition. . . . He was determined to be different and to be noticed."[19] "He often presents," said T. S. Eliot, "the appearance of a man trying to convey to a very deaf person the fact that the house is on fire."[20] Elsewhere, Eliot explains that "half the work that Pound did as a critic can be known only from the testimony of those who have benefitted from his conversation or correspondence."[21]

Pound had his hands in so many pies, and ruffled (and stroked) so many feathers, that one can find a text to prove virtually anything one wants to prove about him. Both the man and his work are complex and difficult. Robert Frost, who neither liked nor trusted him, nevertheless said that "Ezra Pound was the Prime Mover . . . and must always have the credit[,], for what's in it."[22] Ernest Hemingway assured Pound—that "You are the only guy that knows a god damn thing about writing."[23] "Pound was a profoundly good man, of this I am sure," declared the poet Eugenio Montale, speaking from personal knowledge of many years.[24] "Pound has no common sense at all, I would say," wrote G. S. Fraser, "he is a kind of eternal schoolboy."[25] "Mad? He always was eccentric," H.D. put it.[26]

Flaws and all, however, both Pound the man and Pound as a literary figure are noble and enduringly important, taken all in all. We do not need to be hagiographers to understand that comprehension rather than negation is the proper path to follow in dealing with Ezra Pound. Focus on his mistakes, his shortcomings, is petty and in the long run foolish. Focus on his own writing and his own actions and words, further, seems to me the only way to arrive at a consistent comprehension of his six decades of writing and striving. It is Pound's literary career which is central, not the political storm which broke about him after World War Two, when he was arrested and charged with treason, nor the voluminous products of what has been accurately called "the Pound Industry," a vast and apparently unending stream of critical (and uncritical) books and articles annotating and explicating and comparing and contrasting.

Pound deserves to be taken seriously, and he deserves to be taken, as much as possible, on his own terms.

Born in Hailey, Idaho, on 30 October 1885, Ezra Loomis Pound was taken to Philadelphia as a very young child. His grandfather, Thaddeus, made money in the lumber business, was three times elected to Congress from the state of Wisconsin—and late in life separated from his wife and lived, out of wedlock, with "a second feminine adjunct."[27] His personal life is said to have kept him out of President Garfield's cabinet, to which he had been promised nomination. He is also said to have entered Congress rich and to have left it "poor"; it is clear that little or none of his onetime wealth ever descended to Homer Pound, the poet's father, who pretty much made his own way in life. Homer did not do badly: there seems to be no record of how he received his training in matters scientific, but for most of his adult life he served, and lived quite comfortably, as assistant assayer at the United States Mint in Philadelphia. He "was easygoing and seems to have been universally liked," records Pound's best biographer, Noel Stock.[28] Pound described his father as "the naivest man who ever possessed sound sense."[29]

Ezra Pound's boyhood seems to have been essentially normal, for a solidly middleclass boy in that time and that place. There was not a lot of money, but there was a good big house, there were servants, and the family (Pound was an only child) lived well. He visited New York regularly, where his mother's family lived; in the summer of 1898 an aunt took him off on a three-month tour of Europe. He attended private rather than public schools; for some while he boarded at one, the Cheltenham Military Academy, not much more than a mile from his parents' home. In 1901, not quite sixteen years old, he was admitted to the University of Pennsylvania, where he studied for two years; the last two years of his undergraduate work were taken at Hamilton College, in upstate New York, from which he graduated in 1905. In 1905-1907 he did graduate work at the University of Pennsylvania, studying Spanish drama and Spanish literature generally, as well as Latin, Provencal, Old French, and Italian language and literature. He took an M.A. in 1906; for academic 1906-1907 he was appointed a graduate fellow, using the stipend, in the summer of 1906, to make another trip to Europe, working in the libraries of London as well as those in Paris and Madrid. He was planning a doctoral dissertation on the playwright Lope de Vega; it never was written, and Pound never took his Ph.D.

Pound's mother, Isabel, seems to have come from a family of some social and cultural pretension; the Westons seem also to have had serious doubts about her marrying Homer Pound. Homer had "a certain sophistication," Pound tells us, "a certain ability to stand unabashed in the face of the largest national luminaries, to pass the 'ropes', etc., designed for restricting democratic egress."[30] He won the girl he wanted, and they seem to have lived happily together. Isabel participated in reading circles and the like; Stock notes that "with her 'high society' voice, [she] was often regarded as uppish."[31] Writing to her in 1913, apparently in response to a suggestion that he return to the United States, Pound's tone is distinctly defensive, not to say supercilious: "I don't suppose America has more fools per acre than other countries, still your programme of the Ethical Society presents no new argument for my return." And further in the same letter he notes, again apparently in response to reading suggestions from her, that "I can't be bothered to read a novel in 54 vols. Besides I know the man who translated *Jean Christophe*, and moreover it's a popular craze so I suppose something *must* be wrong with it."[32] The next year he writes to her that "It is rather late in the day to go into the whole question of realism in art. I am profoundly pained to hear that you prefer Marie Corelli to Stendhal, but I can not help it."[33]

Pound loved and got on well with his parents; he urged them to come to Europe not only as urgently as they urged him to return to America, but more successfully. When Homer retired, the elder Pounds in fact uprooted themselves and came, lock, stock and barrel, to Italy, as Ezra Pound had wanted. There is no evidence on which to base any significant analysis of Pound's relationship with his parents. There is, however, evidence in his autobiographical essay, "Indiscretions," written about 1921 and first published in 1923, which at least suggests that Pound might have learned from them other things than "virtues . . . as [good] as, or possibly better than . . . intellectual subtlety."[34] Five pages after that comment on his father, Pound notes of logging and similar "menial occupations," that "It, like other labour, is performed by servile classes or by men who simply haven't the brains to do anything else without intolerable mental fatigue, a mental fatigue more torturing than that of the body."[35] Just past the middle of the essay we are offered in a context of historical comment that suggests familial origin, attitudes worthy of a Klu Klux Klansman:

> It must be borne in mind that in the opening of the war for succession the Southern States had probably a "right" to secede, if "right" were to be judged on written documents and on the spirit of the articles of Confederation which preceded the American Constitution. In course of this separatist dispute New York City had mooted secession from the State of New York, and negroes "hung from the lampposts" may have indicated an unwillingness to build black "freedom" on a structure of white slaughter. One of Kipling's characters has summarised the effects of the "War" ('60-65) as extermination of the Anglo-Saxon race in America in order that the Czeko-Slovaks might inherit Boston Common.

This leads immediately into a discussion of the "race-problem," which Pound says "begins where personal friendliness ceases. . . . There are ninety different ways of saying 'Damn nigger'; it requires knowledge to use the right ones. . . . The nigger, like any other fine animal, is very quick to perceive certain tones of personality, of voice, modes of moving, not by cerebral analysis but by 'feel'. Some men never get on with horses; some men are perfect fools in the way they approach any animal." The final paragraph of his disquisition—introduced by a humorous description of an old family servant—makes it clear that Pound is dead serious: "If the old South had not been not only 'destroyed,' but if the actual old white population had not been so

7

definitely, in such actual numbers, killed off and driven away, the 'problem' might be in quieter state and 'solutions' less in demand."[36] It is also true, of course, as anyone who has lived for a time in Philadelphia knows, that the city of Brotherly Love has for many years been a seedbed of racial and religious prejudice. Pound could as easily have acquired attitudes like those I have been quoting on the streets of his native city. But though I cannot prove it, I believe there is some underlying familial origin.

In the fall of 1907, determined not to proceed to the Ph.D., and equally determined "that at thirty I would know more about poetry than any man living,"[37] Pound took a job teaching at Wabash College, in Crawfordsville, Indiana. He pretty much had the run of a department of French, Spanish, and Italian; in two years he could probably have had both a full professorship and a secure tenure. He lasted until November or December of 1907, when he lent his bed to a homeless female actress, stranded and apparently penniless. Pound does not seem to have shared the bed with the lady; he slept on the floor for the night. His landladies found the actress, after Pound had gone off to his teaching duties; it was not long after that the trustees of the college bought off the remainder of his contract and he left Crawfordsville for good.[38] By February 1908, having failed to have a collection of poems published by any American publisher, he took ship for Europe, landing in Gibraltar and proceeding from there to Venice, where he stayed for three months and, at his own expense, printed *A Lume Spento* ("With Tapers Quenched," a title drawn from Dante). Sometime that summer he left Italy, first for France and then, by early fall, for London. He stayed more than a dozen years; when he left for the Continent, in 1921, he took with him a long-established reputation and not a great deal else.

Pound's London years began well. He arrived with next to no money and a few copies of *A Lume Spento*. Within a very short time he had been hired to give a brief course of lectures at the Polytechnic Institute of London on "The Development of Literature in Southern Europe." Introductions regularly led to other introductions: "the town seems to want to treat me white," he wrote to his parents in February 1909.[39] He had met and dined with Laurence Binyon, Maurice Hewlett, May Sinclair, Ernest Rhys, W. B. Yeats, Ford Madox Ford, D. H. Lawrence, Ellen Terry, George Bernard Shaw, Hilaire Belloc, and Sturge Moore. "He had come to England, he later said, to meet William Butler Yeats, whose work he greatly admired; within six months he was meeting everyone."[40] The novelist Olivia Shakespear, married to a prosperous lawyer, and an old flame of Yeats, was both hospitable and helpful; Pound later married her daughter, Dorothy.

A small second volume of poems, *A Quinzaine for This Yule*, appeared in December 1908; like his first book it was privately printed, but unlike his first book it was taken over and reprinted by a recognized British publisher, Elkin Mathews. In January 1909 Mathews accepted his third book, *Personae*, at which time the following famous dialogue took place:

> Mr. E. M.: "Ah, eh, do you care to contribute to the costs of publishing?"
> Mr. E. P.: "I've got a shilling in my clothes, if that's any use to you."
> Mr. E. M.: "Oh well, I rather want to publish 'em anyhow."[41]

Pound began to review for journals, but he was still desperately short of funds. His lectures do not appear to have gone well: "on the day of his fourth lecture, 11 February [1909], he told his father that the series had been ruined by fog."[42] He thought of returning, albeit temporarily, to the United States, to teach. But *Personae* was well received: "Mr. Pound is of the few who have gone forth into life and found something of a new seed," said the *Daily Telegraph* in April 1909;[43] "this book is as tufted with beauty as the bole of an old elm tree with green shoots," said the poet F. S. Flint, writing in the *New Age* in May 1909;[44] "all his poems are . . . in every way, his own, and in a world of his own," wrote the poet Edward Thomas in the *Daily Chronicle*, in June 1909.[45] Pound was signed for a longer series of lectures at the Polytechnic Institute, J. M. Dent (publishers of the Everyman Library) were interested in a book based on the lectures (published in 1910 as *The Spirit of Romance*), Mathews accepted *Exultations*, his fourth book of poems, and things began to run on a slightly steadier keel. By late November 1909, "his name was being mentioned in high company, as when R. B. Cunninghame Graham, in a letter to the *Saturday Review . . .* wrote: 'I observe with pleasure that our best writers—as Conrad, Hudson, Galsworthy, George Moore, Henry James, and Ezra Pound—are devoting themselves more and more to short pieces, and in them doing some of their finest work.' "[46]

His lectures did not go well the second time, either, but he never stopped working in any and every direction available, translating songs for concert singers, taking private students for language lessons, selling poems anywhere he could. In the spring of 1910 he could afford a trip to Paris and then to Verona, where Olivia and Dorothy Shakespear later joined him. In June he sailed for the United States, where he wrote and translated and where, in November, *Provenca*, a book of poems, was for the first time put out by an American publisher. He made fifty dollars for the publication, in Philadelphia's *Sunday School Times,* of a poem entitled "Christmas Prologue." He renewed acquaintance with William Carlos Williams, met and hobnobbed with Yeats's father, and in late February 1911, returned to Europe, not to set foot on American soil for almost thirty years.

Canzoni appeared in 1911, published by Mathews once more: it was the last of his juvenilia, so festooned with archaisms and the like that Ford Madox Ford, handed a copy by the poet, literally rolled on the floor with laughter.[47] Pound was at first shocked, and then—and forever after—profoundly grateful for what he quickly realized was trenchant and basic criticism. His translation of "The Seafarer" from the Old English was perhaps the first concrete evidence that Ford's barbs had gone home: it appeared in November 1911, the first in a twelve-part series of translations and commentaries. H. D. had arrived in London, that year; Pound saw much of her, and of the philosopher (and sometime poet) T. E. Hulme, a cofounder of Imagism. By "the beginning of 1912 Pound was at last launched upon the literary career he had for years looked forward to. He was twenty-six: a tall figure with a shock of yellow-gold hair and a small red beard."[48] He was engaged to Dorothy Shakespear; he was entering on that middle period of his poetic productivity which is, in my opinion, his best period, taken as a whole. By April 1913, the young American writer, Floyd Dell, could declare in the *Chicago Evening Post Literary Review,* "Ezra Pound, we salute you! You are the most enchanting poet alive."[49] Pound had established his immensely important link with Harriet Monroe's new magazine, *Poetry*—and felt himself sufficiently important and established, indeed, to make editorial changes in poems submitted for *Poetry* by no less a figure than W. B. Yeats. Yeats was "astounded at his cheek" (but accepted some of the changes).[50] He felt sufficiently sure of himself, too, to pronounce solemnly that "America has a chance for Renaissance and that certain absurdities in the manners of American action are, after all, things of the surface and not of necessity the symptoms of sterility or even of fatal disease." He could also see resemblances between the "surging crowd" of New York city and the pagan crowds of "imperial Rome . . . eager, careless, with an animal vigour unlike that of any European crowd that I have ever looked at." He could exult, too, that "New York is the most beautiful city in the world!"[51]

Ripostes, published in 1912, is a significant advance over his earlier collections of poetry, though his full breakthrough into the clear, clean lines of his middle period dates from *Lustra* (1916)—and *Lustra* was both preceded and prepared for by his superb retranslations from the Chinese, *Cathay* (1915). Curiously, it was in 1912 also that Arthur Quiller-Couch requested two early poems for his *Oxford Book of Victorian Verse.* (Pound was delighted.)[52] Yeats, on whom Pound was something of an influence during this period, wrote of him in January 1913, that "Ezra . . . is full of the middle ages and helps me to get back to the definite and concrete away from modern abstractions. To talk over a poem with him is like getting you to put a sentence into dialect. All becomes clear and natural. Yet in his own work he is very uncertain, often very bad though very interesting sometimes. He spoils himself by too many experiments and has more sound principles than taste."[53] Others had for some time been saying much the same thing. Edward Thomas, who had

had negative second thoughts, wrote in 1910 that "Mr. Pound
. . . cannot combine the scholar and the man."[54] An anonymous
reviewer declared in 1911 that "Mr. Pound's work is too egotistic
and not individual enough."[55] G. D. H. Cole wrote later that
same year that "Each of his books so far has given us a part of
his genius; some day we hope he will give us all at once."[56]
Pound's friend, F. S. Flint, started a 1912 review of *Canzoni* with
what seemed a ringing declaration: "Let it be conceded at once,
without cavil, that the authentic note of poetry sounds throughout this last book of Mr. Ezra Pound's." But Flint added, at once,
an almost equally ringing caveat: "But is he the instrument, or is
he the wind in the instrument? So much of his inspiration seems
bookish, so much of his attraction lies in the vivid picturesque-
ness of his romance-besprinkled page."[57] Even after *Lustra*, A. R.
Orage—a friendly editor—remarked that "He has always a ton
of precept for a pound of example."[58] Much later on, Louis
Simpson, an American poet almost forty years Pound's junior,
observed trenchantly that "what Pound lacked [as a poet was]
an identity. He had ideas, he had an excellent gift of minicry . . .
but he never had a center of his own."[59] That may be somewhat
severe: closer to the truth, I think, is J. P. Sullivan's more
measured judgment that "Pound is a highly original poet. . . .
There are far more perfect poets, but few responsible for more
innovations."[60] Another way of putting this is to say that
"Whether Pound was making the past his own, or being gob-
bled by the past, is debatable."[61]

Pound's literary discoveries and enthusiasms were being
proclaimed from one end of the world to the other: T. S. Eliot,
James Joyce, Wyndham Lewis, Robert Frost, H.D., the sculptor
Gaudier-Brzeska, and many others. But Pound was already
beginning to close off the possibilities of his London literary
career; he was *too* modern, *too* insistent, *too* careless at times.
"He was unable," says his biographer, Noel Stock, "to handle
with due propriety the multitude of necessary details and in his
letters and his prose showed signs of lapsing more and more
into a private language. He jumped from one point to another
and seldom explained himself."[62] Furthermore, "It was [also] at
this stage that Pound began to have doubts about the turn his

work was taking. While Joyce and Eliot were already producing work that was of the modern world he was playing behind ancient masks, translating Arnaut Daniel again, and in his early cantos worrying out loud about the construction of a suitable 'rag-bag' in which to stuff the modern world but obviously happier when dreaming about the past. . . . His problem was that in his ideas he had consciously developed a modern pro-gramme which seemed to run counter to the ideas and feelings of his sensitive self out of which came his poetry."[63] By 1920, indeed, Louis Untermeyer could writer that "More and more he shrinks back into literature. . . . The library is his ivory tower, and he has locked himself in."[64] It was true, as A. R. Orage said at the time of Pound's departure from London, that "much of the Press has been deliberately closed by cabal to him."[65] It was also true, barely a year later, that "the massive isolation of Ezra Pound has probably not been surpassed by that of any other poet in any other generation, and seldom equalled."[66]

Pound had matured and married in London. He had built a reputation, though not always a positive one; he had laid the financial groundwork for his long years in Italy. T. S. Eliot's Harvard friend, Conrad Aiken (who had in fact been responsi-ble for Eliot's meeting Pound in the first place), wrote in a hostile 1918 review that Pound was "without any doubt a poet who has (sometimes severely) influenced his fellow poets."[67] What had gone wrong? A friendly Italian critic, Emanuel Carnevali, who was briefly on the staff of *Poetry* and who in Pound's own words wrote "about the best" critical articles of the time,[68] said that "Mr. Pound is a gentleman who, possessing a good deal of human discrimination, saw what were the things that a great man is concerned about. Thereupon he laboriously set himself to be concerned in such things."[69] This goes alto-gether too far—but there is truth in it, nevertheless. One of Pound's most devoted friends, Ernest Hemingway, declared ten years later that "Of course Ezra is an ass, but he has written damned lovely poetry. . . . He just makes a bloody fool of himself 99 times out of 100, when he writes anything but poetry, and 40 times out of 100 when he writes poetry."[70]

There is no easy road to the comprehension of Ezra Pound.

I do not pretend that I can explain why his poetry descended into a maelstrom, as he left other things behind and worked away at his *Cantos*—of which long and uncompleted poem that remarkably acute critic, Randall Jarrell, wrote that "What is worst in Pound and what is worst in the age have conspired to ruin the Cantos, and have not quite succeeded."[71] Nor can I explain, neatly and definitively, why he remained in his Italian exile after World War Two broke out, or exactly what he thought he was doing when he broadcast over Italian radio the rambling and probably treasonous material now collected in its entirety for all to read and groan over.[72] I can however make literary sense of his progress as a poet, and of his enormous contribution to the art of translation. I can set forth his critical positions; I can show that, for all their increasingly incoherent general dullness, there are intense flashes of beauty, and of importance, in virtually all the *Cantos*. And despite the hagiographical insistence that at the end of his life Pound did not know what he was saying, when he declared that "I was out of focus,"[73] or that "I have lived all my life believing that I knew something. And then a strange day came and I realized that I knew nothing, that I knew nothing at all. And . . . everything that I touch, I spoil. I have blundered always,"[74] or when he told Allen Ginsberg that "my poems don't make sense,"[75] or said that he had "botched" the *Cantos*, there is truth in these statements, though not the whole truth. Perhaps the whole truth does not exist. "Where are you living now?" a reporter asked him, toward the end of his life. 'In hell,' was Pound's reply. The journalist persisted, 'Which hell?' And the poet, pressing his hands to his heart, mouthed the words, 'Here, here.' "[76]

2 Training and Explorations
The Poetry before *Ripostes*

"I strove a little book to make for her," begins one of Pound's earliest surviving poems—and the words are literal rather than metaphoric. Pound wrote many poems for the young Hilda Doolittle (later to be transformed into the poet H.D.); twenty-five of them he gathered into a small, handbound, handsewn vellum book, mostly typed but in part handwritten, and presented to her as a love token.[1] Four of the poems were later printed in *A Lume Spento*; only "The Tree" was not significantly revised. When however Pound culled his early volumes for the "collected" (in fact "selected") poems now known as *Personae*, none of the "Hilda's Book" entries survived except, again, "The Tree," which was printed as the first poem in *Personae*.

> I strove a little book to make for her.
> Quaint bound, as 'twere in parchment very old,
> That all my dearest words of her should hold,
> Wherein I speak of mystic wings that whirr
> Above me when within my soul do stir
> Strange holy longings
> That may not be told
> Wherein all autumn's crimson and fine gold
> And wold smells subtle as far-wandered myrrh
> Should be as burden to my heart's own song.
> Tho I be weak, is beauty alway strong,
> So be they cup-kiss to the mingled wine
> That life shall pour for us life's ways among.
> *Ecco il libro:* for the book is thine.

The faults of this bookish, stiff, arch, rhetorical, and somewhat pretentious little poem are easy to see—and unimportant.

Neither poets nor poetry as a whole can develop except in stages. What needs to be considered is (a) what was poetry in America like at this period, and (b) how does Pound's juvenile attempt differ, if it does differ, from that prevailing standard? Three of the four final poems in *the* anthology of the time, Stedman's *An American Anthology*, representing what that editor labelled "typical poets and poetry of the [century's] final years," provide a sufficient answer.[2] I give only the title and the first stanza of each.

Gentian
Elizabeth Green Crane

So all day long I followed through the fields
    The voice of Autumn, calling from afar;
And now I thought: "Yon hazel thicket yields
    A glimpse of her," and now: "These asters are
Sure sign that she of late has passed this way;
    Lo! here the traces of her yellow car." . . .

The Parting of the Ways
Joseph B. Gilder

Untrammeled Giant of the West,
    With all of Nature's gifts endowed,
With all of Heaven's mercies blessed,
    Nor of thy power unduly proud—
Peerless in courage, force, and skill,
And godlike in thy strength of will . . .

Dryad Song
Margaret Witter Fuller

I am immortal! I know it! I feel it!
    Hope floods my heart with delight!
Running on air, mad with life, dizzy, reeling,
Upward I mount,—faith is sight, life is feeling,
    Hope is the day-star of might! . . .

16

Set in this context, Pound's poem stands as remarkably individual—the somewhat clotted and derivative but honest and felt expression of real feeling. Pound may be bookish, but Miss Crane is both totally derivative and also devoid of content. Her ear is well schooled, but her poem is intensely trivial. Mr. Gilder's patriotic effusion clamors with a pompousness that makes Pound's mildly pretentious lines sparkle. And Miss Fuller's wildly inane religiosity, supported by no less than five exclamation marks in five lines, makes one wonder how editor Stedman or anyone else could have seen either "taste" or "charm" in her work. Throughout "Hilda's Book," indeed, Pound shows glimpses of rhythmic and phrase-making abilities far beyond anything that Stedman's (and early twentieth-century America's) poetic universe seems able to so much as contemplate.[3] The concluding cadence of the quoted poem rings beautifully clear; the deft use of a phrase from another language (Italian for "here is the book") not only foreshadows much that is to come but "elevates" the poem beyond the commonplace. In a sonnet elsewhere in "Hilda's Book" Pound has two lines that might have come from an "Imagist" volume, ten years down the road: "Thy fingers move again across my face / As little winds that dream." He clots this delicate image with the following line, "But dare in no wise tell their dream aloud," but what matters is the early capability, not the juvenile inability to sustain it.[4] The poem "Era Venuta," retitled "Comraderie" when it appeared in *A Lume Spento*, opens well: "Some times I feel thy cheek against my face / Close pressing." And "The Tree," which still stands at the head of Pound's mature selection of his verse before the *Cantos*, is in some ways more like a ripe lyric by Yeats than, for some years, Yeats himself was able to achieve. There is profound rather than sentimental paganism in the conclusion: "I have been a tree amid the wood / And many new things understood / That were rank folly to my head before."[5]

The five printed volumes, from *A Lume Spento* in 1908 to *Canzoni* in 1911,[6] contained 128 poems. Pound reprinted only thirty-seven of these, or just under twenty-nine percent, when he chose for *Personae*, in 1926, the poems he wanted to keep in print.[7] A full consideration of Pound's juvenilia is beyond either the scope or the intention of this study: I will refer in this chapter principally to the poems Pound elected to keep, though some reference to discarded work will be necessary.

Two or three basic strands run, for good and for bad, through these early poems. Perhaps most obvious to us, now, is the bookish and derivative drawing on older literatures—Greek, Provencal, the poems of Francois Villon, Robert Browning, the Arthurian poets, the poets ɔf Egypt, Dante, Guido Cavalcanti, Propertius, Lucius Apuleius, Du Bellay, Leopardi, A. E. Housman (who is, to be sure, mocked rather than imitated or translated), and Heinrich Heine. This is indeed a list drawn only from the poems surviving in *Personae* (1926): if we go back to the original volumes we need to add Swinburne (to whom the poem "Salve O Pontifex!" is dedicated in *A Lume Spento*), Ernest Dowson, Thomas Beddoes, Agrippa d'Aubigné, Marc Antony Flaminius, Lope de Vega, Pico della Mirandola, Ovid, W. B. Yeats, Old and Middle English poetry, Dante G. Rossetti, Horace, Lionel Johnson, Virgil, Théophile Gautier, Gustave Flaubert, Sappho, Voltaire, Landor, Jonson, Chinese poetry, Henry James, Lord Byron, Shakespeare, Rupert Brooke, Walt Whitman, James Whistler, Catullus, Henri de Régnier, Andrea Navagero, Goethe, Schiller, Ibycus, Martial, Cicero, Hermann Hagedorn, Sir Thomas Malory, Jules Laforgue, and many others.

Virtually all writers learn from those who have gone before them; virtually all writers allude to or imitate or translate from their literary predecessors. And at certain times and certain places these literary connections are stronger and more pervasive than others. The work of T.S. Eliot and Wallace Stevens—to mention only the most prominent among Pound's compatriots and contemporaries—demonstrates that the early years of the twentieth century were distinctly such a time for American writers: Eliot and Stevens are remarkably learned poets and are not shy about exhibiting their learning. But Pound's literary linkages and debts go far beyond anything one can see in Eliot or Stevens; indeed, they probably exceed in both quantity and intensity the linkages and debts to be found in the work of any significant poet one can think of.

Nor can one say simply that the scholar and the poet are deeply intertwined in Pound and in his work. A. E. Housman was as pedantic and rigidly rigorous a scholar as has ever existed; he was also a poet. But though his best recent biography describes him, on its title page, as "The Scholar-Poet," in fact his scholarship had very little to do with his poetry, and vice versa. Ezra Pound was a passionate combiner; Housman never mixed his learning and his verse. Just once, records one of his students, "he looked up at us"—breaking a habit of never looking at his students—"and in quite a different voice said: 'I should like to spend the last few minutes considering this ode [by Horace] simply as poetry'. Our previous experience of Professor Housman would have made us sure that he would regard such a proceeding as beneath contempt." The few moments of passion done with, " 'That', he said hurriedly, almost like a man betraying a secret, 'I regard as the most beautiful poem in ancient literature' and walked quickly out of the room."[8] Pound's devotion to and passion for ancient literature—for literature generally—were the farthest thing from a secret. "Mr. Pound . . . has furious likes and dislikes," wrote G. K. Chesterton approvingly. "He is so much at home in antiquity that he can say he likes Aeschlyus and dislikes Virgil, as you and I might say we like [A's] stories but not [B's] plays."[9] All the same, Housman's poetry is totally independent of his scholarship and Pound's, in these early volumes, is never free of it. "Na Audiart" ("Lady Audiart"), for example, not only has an epigraph in Provencal (*Que be-m vols mal*, "though thou wish me ill," as Pound translates the line later in the poem), but thirteen closely printed lines of preliminary explanation and background. The poem does not sink under its scholastic weight: "Audiart, Audiart, / Where thy bodice laces start / As ivy fingers clutching through / Its crevices." But so much of the poem depends on its borrowed ideas, its borrowed language, its borrowed emotions, that it is hard to say if Pound is its author or, in some odd way, its compiler, its assembler. "Being then young and wry'd, / Broken of ancient pride, / Thou shalt then soften, / Knowing, I know not how, / Thou wert once she / . . . For whose fairness one forgave."[10] The poet responsible for these lines steeped in archaisms was born, remember, in Hailey, Idaho, and raised in Philadelphia; he was writing in the first decade of the twentieth century, not in 1400. The three poets quoted from Stedman's *An American Anthology* are hardly colloquial in tone, but it must be admitted that on this score they do better than Pound, whose bootlaces they are clearly not fit to tie.

Pound drastically improved matters in compiling his 1926 *Personae*. The first poem in *A Lume Spento*, "Grace Before Song," began:

> Lord God of heaven that with mercy dight
> Th'alternate prayer wheel of the night and light
> Eternal hath to thee, and in whose sight
> Our days as rain drops in the sea surge fall . . .

The poem was dropped, as it deserved to be. The second poem in *A Lume Spento*, "La Fraisne" ("The Ash Tree"), has survived Pound's drastic pruning—but as late as 1920, somewhat surprisingly, it was still prefaced by its original page of prefatory comment and explanation. As a pseudo-Browningesque dramatic monologue it lacks either force or conviction. "Once there was a woman . . . / . . . but I forget . . . she was . . . / . . . I hope she will not come again. / / . . . I do not remember." This is not only mechanical and essentially empty as well as derivative, but it is also, as the more mature Pound stroke never to be, tautological: "I do not remember" flails and strains, for anything it has to say has already been said with "but I forget." But the poem is nonetheless improved by omitting the prefatory matter. "Fifine Answers," another Browning imitation, was sensibly omitted from *Personae*. "Sharing his exile that hath borne the flame, / Joining his freedom that hath drunk the shame / And known the torture of the Skull-place hours / Free and so bound, that mingled with the powers / Of air and sea and light." Pound's mimetic talents are so great that what he imitates, here, are Browning's eccentricities; he catches the clotted awkwardness beautifully. But is the game worth the candle? More: is it intended to be more than a clever game? Poets must practice, if they are to mature in their craft, but Pound's muscle-testing and flexing is too pronounced to be satisfactory. It is not so much that reality escapes him in many of these poems, but rather that in such poems he does not seem even to try to capture reality.

And yet his mimetic bent also enabled him to produce, even in *A Lume Spento,* two appreciations of Francois Villon that capture, as almost nothing else in English does, the deepest tones and much of the power of that rollicking old French poet:

> Towards the Noel that morte saison
> (*Christ make the shepherds' homage dear!*)
> Then when the grey wolves everychone
> Drink of the winds their chill small-beer
> And lap o' the snows food's gueredon*
> Then makyth my heart his yule-tide cheer
> (Skoal! with the dregs if the clear be gone!)
> Wineing the ghosts of yester-year.

There is no French original for this poem, "Villonaud for This Yule." Pound has so steeped himself not only in archaisms, but in the driving spirit of Villon's poetry, that he is able to magnificently echo it, recreate it. He is an important force in the history of translation—but this is not translation. It is of course not written in the language of 1908, but it was not meant to be.

Nor is archaic, derivative language all we find, even in *A Lume Spento.* "Famam Librosque Cano" ("I sing of fame and books," aping Virgil's *Aeneid,* "Arma virumque cano," "Arms and the man I sing") is blessed with its share of Browningisms, and uses such forms as "shrinketh" and "sith" and "scaped." But it opens with three lines that anticipate "Hugh Selwyn Mauberley" (1920), one of Pound's finest mature poems: "Your songs? / Oh! The little mothers / Will sing them in the twilight." So consistently clean and straightforward a style eluded Pound for many years, but when he found it there could be no question of its origins in his own earlier work. So too "The Eyes" (originally titled "The Cry of the Eyes") is for four of its five strophes in the style that has been called "Pound's stiff-wristed Rossetti-and-Swinburne lyrics and Browning-and-sugar-water monologues."[11] But the fourth strophe breaks away:

---

*gueredon = reward

> Free us, for we perish
> In this ever-flowing monotony
> Of ugly print marks, black
> Upon white parchment.

Pound was only twenty-three and he could not sustain such passages. But they are there, and he wrote them. There is surely a conflict between his modernist poetic theories and pronouncements and much if not most of the actual poetry he was then producing. "Make it new" has always been Pound's battle cry, though he did not expressly use that phrase as a title until 1934. But in a prescriptive essay first published in 1913 he declared "Use no superfluous word. . . . Go in fear of abstractions. Do not retell in mediocre verse what has already been done in good prose. . . . Be influenced by as many great artists as you can, but have the decency either to acknowledge the debt outright, or try to conceal it. . . . Use either no ornament or good ornament."[12] A year earlier he had said that "I believe in technique as the test of a man's sincerity," and then in 1917 that "If a certain thing was said once for all in Atlantis or Arcadia, in 450 Before Christ or in 1290 after, *it is not for us moderns to go saying it over,* or to go obscuring the memory of the dead by saying the same thing with less skill and less conviction" (italics added).[13] Resolving the conflict between approach and performance was a lifelong struggle for Pound; he had neither settled the issue nor either won or lost the struggle when he died.

But there is a good deal more to the conflict than simple reliance, even excessive reliance, on the work of earlier poets. Let me return to "Grace Before Song," the first poem in *A Lume Spento*—dropped when *Personae* was put together in 1926—and reproduce it entire:

> Lord God of heaven that with mercy dight
> Th'alternate prayer wheel of the night and light
> Eternal hath to thee, and in whose sight
> Our days as rain drops in the sea surge fall,
>
> As bright white drops upon a leaden sea
> Grant so my songs to this grey folk may be:

As drops that dream and gleam and falling catch the sun,
Evan'scent mirrors every opal one
Of such his splendor as their compass is,
So, bold My Songs, seek ye such death as this.

It is derivative, archaic, and not very good; it is also exceedingly romantic. The poet wishes his poems to be "as bright white drops upon a leaden sea" to ordinary mortals, who are in his view "grey folk." He wishes his poems to "dream and gleam"; there is also a rather Wagnerian "love-death" motif, in which beauty and love are linked with "falling" into the sea and "death." It is impossible to say whether Pound wrote romantically because he was overly influenced by and overly fond of his poetic predecessors, or whether he wrote archaically because he was decidedly a romantic—and there is no need to thus simplify and dispose of the matter. The fact is that romanticism runs through all of his early poetry; it is the second of the basic strands readily visible in that early verse.

Passing over *A Quinzaine for This Yule* (1908), from which only one poem survived into *Personae* (1926), we find in the first of his two books entitled *Personae*, published in 1909, five poems that Pound later chose to preserve; of these five only one is not decidedly romantic—and that one, "Marvoil," is an exploration of the inner nature of the Provencal poet, Arnaut de Mareuil (fl. 1170–1200). "In Durance," which Pound dates 1907 (it was probably written during his brief tenure at Wabash College), is less a complaint that "I am homesick after mine own kind" than a hymn to beauty and to those who, like the poet, worship at Beauty's shrine.

> And yet my soul sings "Up!" and we are one.
> Yea thou, and Thou, and THOU, and all my kin
> To whom my breast and arms are ever warm,
> For that I love ye as the wind the trees
> That holds their blossoms and their leaves in cure
> And calls the utmost singing from the boughs
> That 'thout him . . . were as dumb
> Still shade . . . "

"The White Stag"—the image is drawn from Malory's *Morte Darthur* (III, 5)—is short enough to reproduce in its entirety:

> I ha' seen them 'mid the clouds on the heather.
> Lo! they pause nor for love nor for sorrow,
> Yet their eyes are as the eyes of a maid to her lover,
> When the white hart breaks his cover
> And the white wind breaks the morn.
>
> " *'Tis the white stag, Fame, we're a-hunting,*
> *Bid the world's hounds come to horn!"*

It would be hard to be, at one and the same time, more literary and more romantic. The Tennysonian fourth and fifth lines are handled beautifully; the apostrophe to fame with which the poem ends is passionately meant. Indeed, in the final strophe of "And Thus in Nineveh," in which in *Personae* (1926) Pound altered the biblical-sounding Raama (see Genesis 10:7) to the Norse Raana, literary romanticism is formulated in the clearest, most elitist terms:

> "It is not, Raana, that my song sings highest
> Or more sweet in tone than any, but that I
> Am here a Poet, *that doth drink of life*
> *As lesser men drink wine.*"

The italics are mine rather than Pound's: I use them to highlight what seems to me in some ways the most significant phrase in all his early verse. Putting his words in the mouth of an imaginary Assyrian poet, Pound declares first that the quality of his poetry is of no importance, and second that what really matters is simply and solely being a poet, a creature who by that very fact of vocation (and of course the ability to practice that vocation) is able to savor life "as lesser men drink wine."

There is evidence, too—and this leads to the third of the basic strands in his early poetry—that Pound took his own dictum very much to heart. In the last of this early volume's poems to be preserved in *Personae* (1926), "Praise of Ysolt," he flails rather wordily at the notion that though all the world calls to him for songs, "I cried unto them 'I have no song / For she I

24

sang of hath gone from me.' " It is both the most romantic and the most confused of the poems surviving from this early volume, but it is probably not addressed to some impersonal muse, as those who have noticed the poem at all have thought, but to H.D., his onetime inamorata.[14] Ysolt, or Isolde, is the great love of Tristram (or Tristan); the editor of "Hilda's Book" informs us that there are many "early poems addressed to Hilda [Doolittle] (as 'Is-hilda' or 'Ysolt').[15] "My song was ablaze with her," Pound writes, "and she went from me / As flame leaveth the embers." Before giving us poems from *Ripostes* (1912—to be considered in chapter three), Pound has fifty poems in *Personae* (1926), counting the various Heine versions, this time, as separate poems. I count twenty-three that are not about matters of love and sex (of which eleven are about poetry), and twenty-seven that are about love and sex. I have not bothered to count and classify the poems in the five volumes of original poetry from which these fifty have been culled; Pound's own selection weights the scales sufficiently clearly. "I have sung women in three cities," he makes his persona declare in "Cino" (the fourteenth-century Italian poet, Cino da Pistoia).

Pound's relationship with Hilda Doolittle is not the subject of all these poems, but even without full biographical knowledge there are clear signs that Pound's concern with love and sex was hardly limited to literary expression. It is well known that, even before his wife gave birth to Pound's son, Omar, Pound's longtime mistress, the violinist Olga Rudge, gave birth to Pound's daughter, Mary (now Mary de Rachewiltz and the author of a fascinating memoir of her relationship with her father).[16] Pound's biographer records that he and Bride Scratton "were very close . . . and saw a good deal of each other," adding discretely that when she was sued for divorce in 1923 "her husband . . . named Pound as co-respondent."[17] Heymann says flatly that "in his life . . . women had always come and gone (both Yeats and Joseph Conrad could testify to the heavy *Verkehr* [sexual traffic, activity])."[18] In short, without needing to dot all the i's and cross all the t's, it is plain that Pound was Bohemian in both word and deed. The significance of that fact, if it has any, is surely that Pound's life and his art were more closely interwoven, at this period, than has usually been realized. Pound's economics, and his peculiar perspectives on American history and Italian fascism, obviously dominate much if not most of the *Cantos:* life and art are there intermingled without any doubt. But the same must, though in different terms, be said of the poetry and the poet's life up to about 1920.

There is possibly a larger significance to this intermingling of life and art, this intertwining of poems about romance and romantic actions. Pound was over thirty, and already the author of five volumes of original verse, two of translations, and of a good deal of critical and journalistic prose, before he published *Lustra* (1916) and finally, fully found, to the extent he ever found it, the clear, direct voice that said without interference what he wanted to say in a voice of his own. It was a relatively slow maturation, especially for a poet of such dedication and of such intense productivity. There are other poets who have matured slowly, notably W. B. Yeats, but it is in general the exception rather than the rule. Nor did Pound succeed in holding onto, or in developing, the clear voice he had found for himself with *Lustra* (and through the aid of his Chinese translations, in *Cathay*, 1915). Neither his ambitions nor his sense of values would allow him to work any longer with the voice or the themes of "Mauberley" (which I take to be his best poetry, all in all), and on he plunged, into the never-finished and I think intrinsically unfinishable *Cantos*. If, then, we consider this man of superb literary skills, blessed with overflowing energy but inexplicably stalled in a long preliminary state, bound over-closely to his literary forebears, afflicted with archaic language from which he only slowly broke himself (and not perma-nently—the *Cantos* are full of archaisms), and both in his poetry and in his personal life deeply swept up in matters romantic, we can begin to see at least the beginning of a pattern. Add, too, Pound's lifelong restlessness, his inability to focus and his simultaneous need to always explore new boundaries, new disciplines, new places, and the pattern may come still clearer. Pound, says J. P. Sullivan, "is not concerned with any deeper spiritual reality"—recall Pound's statement that "I believe in technique as the test of a man's sincerity"—and so, though he *"felt* as strongly as, say, Eliot, . . . his perception was not so sharp, nor could he realize its implications so broadly. . . . Pound could express anything he felt and his expression of things seen was equally adequate, but neither his visual range nor his mental conceptions are in general superlative."[19] Sullivan is not saying simply that Pound had limitations, as of course we all do, but that his limitations were of a very special order. There has always been some question about Pound as an integrated, fully unified personality; one critic, and perhaps others, has gone so far as to assert that "the Pound *within* the great vortex of energy and creation does not exist."[20] Though there is no need to go to such lengths, certainly all the evidence, poetic and personal, suggests a man, and therefore a poet, in part split by unresolvable tensions, inner conflicts which for whatever reason life and its experience were unable ever to quite resolve. This is not to denigrate either Pound or his achievement, but only to help explain why, at the end of his life, he could say, "out of the blue, in a Learlike moan, *"I have never made a person happy in my life,"*[21] and why he could at about the same time say of his poetry that it was "a mess. . . . My writing—stupidity and ignorance all the way through . . . stupidity and ignorance."[22] One could say, as Heymann does, that "he had simply taken on too much, become too multiple, wasting himself in the process, dispersing himself beyond his human limitations."[23] But perhaps, to put it in a different perspective, Pound could not help himself, being all his life uncertain where his true center was, and forever thrashing about in a passionate, honest, but unsuccessful attempt to find that center.

The poems in *Exultations* (1909), of which six are preserved in *Personae* (1926), mark no great forward advance. "Ballad of the Goodly Fere" ("fere" is glossed by Pound himself as "Mate, Companion") is in a vein similar to that of the Villonesque poems discussed earlier in this chapter. It shows what Pound could do as a mimetic adaptor—but he was capable of almost anything, in that vein. "Guido Invites You Thus" is a fine evocation of Guido Cavalcanti; it carries Pound no farther along the road of Browning-like dramatic monologues than do other poems surviving from this volume, "Piere Vidal Old," "Planh for the young English King," and "Sestina: Altaforte." These are polished poems of considerable accomplishment; they are not either "modern" or in a voice in any way identifiably Pound's own. The last surviving poem from this volume, "Francesca," has sometimes been taken as a Rossetti-like effusion, essentially pre-Raphaelite in inspiration. I take it, instead, as a small but significant step toward the plangency of "Mauberley" and of *Lustra* generally:

> You came in out of the night
> And there were flowers in your hands,
> Now you will come out of a confusion of people,
> Out of a turmoil of speech about you.
>
> I who have seen you amid the primal things
> Was angry when they spoke your name
> In ordinary places.
> I would that the cool waves might flow over my mind,
> And that the world should dry as a dead leaf,
> Or as a dandelion seed-pod and be swept away,
> So that I might find you again,
> Alone.

The language is literary rather than colloquial, much of the imagery too is literary, but there seems to be some genuine experience behind the poem—and though literary, the language is distinctly unarchaic. Pound does not seem quite at home with straightforward, natural syntax, or with words of exclusively modern flavor, but for all that it is a step in the right direction, the direction later to be taken.

Eleven poems were culled from *Canzoni* (1911), the volume which rolled Ford Madox Ford on the floor in uproarious laughter. The first poem in the book, not reprinted, begins "Ah! red-leafed time hath driven out the rose. And crimson dew is fallen on the leaf / Ere ever yet the cold white wheat be sown / That hideth all earth's green and sere and red." One can see why Ford was amused: this is material that Stedman might have considered for his anthology, so blandly derivative and archaic is it. But after no less than thirty-one poems in much the same manner (eight of the best of which Pound chose to preserve, in whole or in part, in *Personae)*, we come to, first, "Mr. Housman's Message" (orginally entitled "Song in the Manner of Housman"), and then, as the volume's penultimate entry, seven "Translations from Heine" (which in *Personae* became eight "translations and adaptations") plus a four-line poem, "Translator to Translated." The short original poem is hardly remarkable, but the spoof of Housman is beautifully savage: "O woe, woe, / People are born and die, / We also shall be dead pretty soon / Therefore let us act as if we were dead already." And this *is* colloquial language, with all the snap and sparkle both of good prose and of real speech. The poem would be a significant signpost even if it occurred alone. But it is not alone, for the Heine versions also feature straightforward syntax, colloquial language—and no matter what anyone says, they also capture better than any versions I know the true, racy flavor of Heine. I will discuss Pound as a translator in chapter four, but one example must be set out now. Here is the German for Pound's version number four (it is in fact the first of thirteen stanzas, in the original):

> Mir träumt': ich bin der liebe Gott,
> Und sitz' im Himmel droben,
> Und Englein sitzen um mich her,
> Die meine Verse loben.

John Todhunter's academic version has the sense right, but very little else:

> I dreamt I was the Lord Himself,
>   Throned up in heaven so grandly,
> With sweet young angels round my throne
>   Who praised my verses blandly.

"Im Himmel droben" means "up there in Heaven": the grandly / blandly rhyme is the translator's labored invention. "Englein" are "little angels"; there is no "sweet" in the German. Nor is there any "throne" in line three. Pound's version lexically renders the original far better, but before we get to Pound, consider Aaron Kramer's competent translation:

> I dreamed: I am the dear Lord God
> Enthroned in Heaven's palace:
> The angels sit surrounding me
> And sweetly praise my ballads.

This comes a good deal closer to the nature of Heine's German, but would that poet have the reputation he has if his poetry were in truth like this? Here then is Pound:

> I dreamt that I was God Himself
> Whom heavenly joy immerses,
> And all the angels sat about
> And praised my verses.

This is actually no freer with the German than either of the other translations. But Pound's freedom is meaningful, he departs from the original in order to accomplish something, namely, the beautiful Heine-like rhyme of immerses/verses. More important for our discussion in this chapter, Pound has hit on a delicacy, a lightness of tone that neither of the other translators (nor many poets of the time, whether translating or not) can match. It is not yet his own poetry, nor is it consistently managed even in the next volume, *Ripostes* (1912), but this is yet another significant step taken, another stage reached.

3 Maturity and Beyond
The Poetry Collected in *Personae* (1926)

Ripostes (1912) is Pound's transitional volume, in which he moves decisively away from his earliest approaches and begins to clarify and formulate what will shortly become his high middle style, culminating in "Mauberley" (1920). Significantly, of the twenty-five poems appearing in *Ripostes*, only two were not chosen by Pound for *Personae* (1926)—by far the highest retention rate for any of the first six volumes of original verse, only two of which, *Exultations* and *Canzoni*, exceed (and just barely exceed) a fifty percent survival rate. It will be worth our while, accordingly, to begin consideration of *Ripostes* by briefly looking at these two rejected poems: what Pound did not want to preserve will be helpful when we examine what he did choose to keep.

"Echoes" is a two-part poem, twenty-nine lines in all, which begins with "Guido Orlando, singing," and what he sings is: "Befits me praise thine empery, Lady of Valour, / Past all disproving; / Thou art the flower to me— / / Nay, by Love's pallor— / Of all good loving." And so on, for fifteen lines. It is not only exceedingly archaic, but mechanical and sterile as well. Pound did well to eliminate what was plainly a backward rather than a forward movement. The poem's second part, similarly, begins "Thou keep'st thy rose-leaf / Till the rose-time will be over, / Think'st thou that Death will kiss thee?" There is no need to quote more: part two is much the same as part one, and neither represents anything that had not been thoroughly exhausted by earlier verse.

The second omitted poem, "Effects of Music Upon a Company of People," is both longer and more interesting. Again in two parts, the first subdivided into sections of fifteen and of thirteen lines, the second of nineteen more or less continuous lines, the poem is an experiment, almost more in the mode of William Carlos Williams (to whom *Ripostes* was dedicated) than that of Pound himself. Visual presentation of music and its effects is the subject matter, though it remains somewhat nebulous: the first part is labelled "deux mouvements" (two movements), the second "From a Thing by Schumann." The poem is labored, artificial, and unconvincing, which is surely why Pound dropped it in compiling *Personae* (1926). We hear of "souls like petals" which curl "Pale green, pale gold, transparent, / Green of plasma, rose-white, / Spirate like smoke." This hardly evokes what Pound calls, in the last line of the first subsection of part one, a "crowd of foolish people." In fact, it evokes nothing much of anything. But the experiment is a serious one and worth making. The second subsection of part one, similarly, has a controlling dance motif; we hear of "Woven the step, / Woven the tread, the moving," but again very little is actually communicated. Part two is also full of "floating and welling"; there is some dissociated sea and storm imagery, but nothing connects, it is all the same abstract, disembodied series of movement and color words. The fact that Pound included the poem in his book tells us a good deal about the uncertainty of his standards in 1912; the fact that he omitted it later tells us a good deal about how far he had come in the interim.

The first poem in *Ripostes*, "Silet," assures us that Pound has come a very long way in the year since his previous volume, *Canzoni*. The poem begins:

> When I behold how black, immortal ink
> Drips from my deathless pen—ah, well-away!
> Why should we stop at all for what I think?
> There is enough in what I chance to say.

The language is still on the stiff side, and the basic conceit is more than a little derivative. But the syntax is straightforward and contemporary, and the ironic stance is directed at himself (instead of, say, Housman), producing a healthy measure of the distancing so needed in much of Pound's early work. Looking back four years later, he himself saw that "in the 'search for oneself', in the search for 'sincere self-expression', one gropes, one finds some seeming verity. One says 'I am' this, that, or the other, and with the words scarcely uttered one ceases to be that thing." He also commented that "in reading over what I have written [his *Gaudier-Brzeska* tribute] I find it full of conceit, or at least full of pronouns in the first person." And he sums up by noting that "I began this search for the real in a book called *Personae* [1909], casting off, as it were, complete masks of the self in each poem. I continued in a long series of translations, which were but more elaborate masks." The quotation marks Pound places around phrases like "search for oneself" and "sincere self-expression," as well as the affirmation "I am," clearly indicate his uncertainty in these matters. His shrinking away from the first person singular pronoun reinforces that plain uncertainty for us; the notion of employing a succession of masks, each different but each yet another disguise of the self, reinforces it still further. And when he goes on to speak of a poem which has "an objective reality," we must be quite fully aware that Pound knew pretty well what his problem was.[1] The question remained, of course, what to do about it, how to solve it, if a solution was possible.

"All poetic language is the language of exploration," Pound asserts in *Gaudier-Brzeska*[2]—but given his conflicted nature, as both man and poet, the assertion somewhat begs the question. Exploration, yes, but of what? "Silet" (meaning "he is silent") is a modest poem, a quiet sonnet on the transitoriness of sexual affection and pleasure. "It is enough that we once came together; / What is the use of setting it to rime?" There is perhaps something of the manner of Jules Laforgue here, a deliberately trivializing self-mockery that does not seem fully natural to Pound.[3] "Silet" does not explore very far or very venturesomely: the techniques of straightforwardness and irony are still too new to Pound to permit their full use. The same must be said of the following poem, "In Exitum Cuiusdam"; note that the poem's epigraph is a translation of this title. Nor do we find much deepening in "The Tomb at Akr Caar," a soul-and-body monologue spoken to a now mummified corpse. But in " Portrait d'une Femme" (Portrait of a Lady) we come on a poem almost fully mature—not Pound at his deepest or most rapier-like swiftness, but clear and consistently contemporaneous in language, and carefully textured.

> You have been second always. Tragical?
> No. You preferred it to the usual thing:
> One dull man, dulling and uxorious,
> One average mind—with one thought less, each year.

Pound has cadenced the poem with a fine intermixture of long and short phrases, a delicate blend of sweeping movement and abrupt halts. To emphasize just how far he has come in only four years, let me set out once again the first four lines of the first poem in *A Lume Spento*, "Grace Before Song":

> Lord God of heaven that with mercy dight
> Th'alternate prayer wheel of the night and light
> Eternal hath to thee, and in whose sight
> Our days as rain drops in the sea surge fall . . .

It is as hard to place this sort of thing in the twentieth century as it is to place "Portrait d'une Femme" anywhere else:

> and yet
> For all this sea-hoard of deciduous things,
> Strange woods half sodden, and new brighter stuff:
> In the slow float of differing light and deep,
> No! there is nothing! In the whole and all,
> Nothing that's quite your own.
> Yet this is you.

There is sufficient formality of technique and rhetorical tone that Edward Marsh, friend and later biographer of Rupert Brooke, wanted to include the poem in his anthology of *Georgian Poetry, 1911–1912*. Pound turned the idea down on the grounds that he was including the poem in a book of his own and that neither "Portrait d'une Femme" nor "Ballad of the Goodly Fere" "illustrate[d] any modern tendency."[4] But Marsh was correct: Pound had not yet broken totally free and become the poetic radical that his critical writing, but not yet his actual verse, spoke of.

Yet another partial resolution of conflict and difference appears in "N.Y.," namely Pound's coming to relative peace with Walt Whitman. The process was to be essentially completed the next year, when he wrote in "A Pact" that "I make a pact with you, Walt Whitman— / I have detested you long enough. / . . . We have one sap and one root— / Let there be commerce between us."[5] Pound had been deeply ambivalent about the man he called in 1909 "America's poet . . . the only one of the conventionally recognized 'American Poets' who is worth reading. . . . His crudity is an exceeding great stench, but it *is* America. . . . He is disgusting. He is an exceedingly nauseating pill, but he accomplishes his mission. . . . And yet if a man has written lines like Whitman's to the *Sunset Breeze* one has to love him. . . . Mentally I am a Walt Whitman who has learned to wear a collar and a dress shirt . . . yet with a lesser vitality as I am the more in love with beauty (If I really do love it more than he did)."[6] In 1910 he had written of "that horrible air of rectitude with which Whitman rejoices in being Whitman. . . . [He] pretend[s] to be conferring a philanthropic benefit on the race by recording his own self-complacency."[7] Even in 1913 he wrote to his father that "Whitman is a hard nutt. The *Leaves of Grass* is the book. It is impossible to read it without swearing at the author almost continuously."[8] Before *Ripostes* there is virtually no trace of Whitman in Pound's poetry; beginning with that volume, however, Whitman is regularly encountered, whether named or not. And "N.Y.," though it is neither a particularly good poem nor Whitman fully absorbed, marks the start of that process: "My City, my beloved, my white! Ah, slender, / Listen! Listen to me, and I will breathe into thee a soul. / Delicately upon the reed, attend me!" "The Plunge," perhaps in part addressed to his fiancée, Dorothy Shakespear, is better:

> You, I would have flow over me like water,
> Oh, but far out of this!
> Grass, and low fields, and hills,
> And sun,

> Oh, sun enough!
> Out, and alone, among some
> Alien people!

This is a good deal less obtrusively Whitman, and a good deal more like the mature Pound, now coming to the fore. (Again, he was twenty-seven when *Ripostes* appeared.)

Another ancestor, Old English (or Anglo-Saxon) verse, is taken in hand, too. Pound's "The Seafarer" is both justly famous and an important step toward his own conquest of the blunt, hard phrase, the swift, pounding rhythm of modern speech. It is important to understand just what Pound does and does not do with the Old English text. It is the sound, the musical movement, the clashing alliteration and the harsh consonantal grinding that he is after, and no one before or since has caught in modern English so much of the genuine aural atmosphere of Old English:

> May I for my own self song's truth reckon,
> Journey's jargon, how I in harsh days
> Hardship endured oft.
> Bitter breast-cares have I abided,
> Known on my keel many a care's hold

What Pound does not do—does not try to do—is translate in the usual sense of that word. That is, the verbal meaning, as opposed to the verbal music, is of minimal importance to him. When it becomes necessary to slight, or even to discard, lexical significance in order to produce the aural effects he is after, he does not hesitate. "Journey's jargon," for example, is pretty much empty of meaning: if it does signify anything in modern English it would be something like "the specialized language of travelling." The Old English, however, is "sithas secgan," or "tell of journeys," which is, to say the least, very different. To "abide" sorrows (or "breast-cares") is basically comprehensible. The Old English is much more specific: the verb rendered as "abided" is in fact "gebiden," which means "endured, experienced." I suspect it is possible, by thinking metaphorically, to speak of a man's "keel"—that is, perhaps, a man who sails in a ship. But this is neither exact modern usage nor an exact rendering of the original, which says "gecunnad in ceole," or "experienced in/on ship." Similarly, "many a care's hold" is tangentially related both to modern and to the original Old English, which reads "cearselda fela," or "many places of sorrow."

But Pound's purpose in rendering "The Seafarer" as he does is still more complex, for his vision of the sensibility behind the poem does not entirely square with what the text says. Pound therefore takes two "meaning" oriented steps to bring that text into line: (1) he suppresses the last twenty-five lines, which are an unmistakable prayer, and (2) at every point where a word has religious intent he turns it into a secular word. Pound's "Seafarer," accordingly, is rigorously this-world oriented, rigorously secular. There is in fact some scholarly uncertainty about the last part of the Old English text—but not on the grounds that it is religious, but only that it may (or may not) be an addition to some lost original still older than the poem we have. The best modern edition, that by I. L. Gordon, admits the uncertainty but concludes that the ending "makes a fitting concluding summary of the whole homiletic theme."[9] There is literally *no* scholar of Old English who sees "The Seafarer" as a secular poem. When therefore Pound renders line forty-three, "to hwon hine dryhten gedon wille," he produces "Whatever his lord will." But "dryhten" here is either Fate, in a non-Christian but religious sense, or God, in a Christian sense. "His lord" is simply wrong—not that Pound worries about such things, or indeed that he ought to worry about them, for as I shall make clear in the next chapter Pound's view of translation is appropriative, not scholarly. Nor do I mean to criticize him for that view, to which in my judgment he is more than entitled. I want only to set the record absolutely straight. Pound translated "The Seafarer," as I suspect he translated virtually everything he brought over into English from some other tongue, for his own purposes and for his own use. Once we understand that, we can give over the empty arguments that have been conducted, as pro-Pound and anti-Pound warriors have fought around and around the fields and meadows of Poundian translation.

Just as Pound sharpened his command of rugged language, in translating from the Old English, so too in "Δωρια" ("Doria") he asserted substantively rugged positions—especially rugged in view of the consistent romanticism of his earliest poetry. K. K. Ruthven says that in this little poem—the Greek title is ambiguous, possibly meaning "a gift," possibly meaning "in the Dorian manner," possibly being a reference to Dorothy Shakespear—Pound "rejected the transient attractions of romantic love in favor of something that is closer to harsh reality and therefore more likely to be durable."[10] But the language as well is tougher, leaner:

> Be in me as the eternal moods
> of the bleak wind, and not
> As transient things are—
> gaiety of flowers.
> Have me in the strong loneliness
> of sunless cliffs
> And of grey waters.
> Let the gods speak softly of us
> In days hereafter,
> The shadowy flowers of Orcus*
> Remember thee.

Pound's desire to have poetry "as much like granite as it can be"[11] becomes something more than mere precept, in poems like this. The rhetorical tone is controlled, sparse; the rhythms are strong—not unlyrical so much as securely powerful. The prosody too is securely measured, in units very speechlike, composed "in the sequence of the musical phrase, not in sequence of a metronome. . . . Your rhythmic structure," Pound cautioned, "should not destroy the shape of your words, or their natural sound, or their meaning. . . . I believe in an 'absolute rhythm', a rhythm, that is, in poetry which corresponds exactly to the emotion or shade of emotion to be expressed. A man's rhythm must be interpretative, it will be, therefore, in the end, his own, uncounterfeiting, uncounterfeitable."[12] Pound is probably more

---

*Orcus = hell, the underworld of death

scientific than is warranted in these rigorous formulations; though he declared, in 1913 and thereafter, that "The arts, literature, poesy, are a science, just as chemistry is a science,"[13] the assertion is valuable principally as an indication of its author's state of mind. Bluntly, the arts are neither a science nor comparable to chemistry; neither Pound nor some of those who proclaim allegiance to his banner seem aware, sometimes, that mere statement does not create inalienable truth. But when Pound turned away from older metrical conventions, and towards what is misleadingly called "free verse"—meaning, of course, no more than verse which is cadenced according to variable rather than according to fixed patterns—he expressed an immensely meaningful attitude. In poems like this he actualizes those attitudes: this is performance, not mere precept. And it fully justifies Pound's insistence on the "immorality of bad art," which is "inaccurate art," or "art that makes false reports." What he calls "the art of diagnosis" or "the cult of ugliness," on the one hand, and "the art of cure" or "the cult of beauty" on the other, are thus "not in mutual opposition" but working through different means to the same end, the "good art . . . that bears true witness."[14] It is in this sense, too, that his fine 1918 essay on Henry James identifies James as a "hater of tyranny," a fighter "against all the sordid petty personal crushing oppression . . . of modern life."[15] (I will return to these matters later in this chapter and again in chapter five, on Pound's literary and social criticism.)

Ripostes brought Pound to the edge of his mature middle style; there were many things and many people which helped bring him the rest of the way, by the time of *Lustra* (1916). His reading in modern French poets helped; his friendship with T. S. Eliot, which began in 1914—Pound declared Eliot "the only American I know of who has made what I can call adequate preparation for writing. He has actually trained himself *and* modernized himself *on his own*"[16]—was critically important. His translations from the Chinese, published as *Cathay* (1915), were extremely valuable training, though it is claiming too much to say that working on these poems "gave him a sudden liberation from the linguistic bondage he had imposed upon himelf all these years."[17] On the evidence of Pound's five early volumes, and then of *Ripostes*, it seems to me that we have no choice but to admit that Pound, too, "has actually trained himself *and* modernized himself." If he has not quite managed it, as Eliot had, *"on his own,"* he has certainly made excellent use of all the assistance available. Nor ought we to forget the role of ordinary maturation: Pound was twenty-three when *A Lume Spento* was published, but past thirty when *Lustra* appeared.

There are far too many poems in the sections of *Personae* (1926) entitled "Lustra," "Poems from Blast," and "Poems from Lustra," plus the few poems added as "Early Poems, Not Previously Collected . . . ," for full discussion of each and all. In the remainder of this chapter I will necessarily highlight and abbreviate, and I will necessarily omit: my aim is to indicate the outlines of Pound's mature middle style, and to focus on "Mauberley."

Pound plunges right in: the first poem in *Lustra*, "Tenzone" (Provencal for a verse debate between rival troubadors), begins: "Will people accept them? / (i.e. these songs), / As a timorous wench from a centaur / (or a centurion), / Already they flee, howling in terror. / . . . Their virgin stupidity is untemptable." The question is plainly rhetorical; Pound is very sure indeed that the answer is that they will not accept such songs as these new ones of his. The last strophe slips back a bit into something slightly resembling "And Thus in Ninevah," with its rhapsodic declarations of the poet's intrinsic superiority: "I mate with my free kind upon the crags." But the poem *is* very different, not only in the condensed sharpness of its irony, but even more in the swaggering confidence of its colloquial language. Pound has asserted confidence, earlier; he has never before attained such polished, deft arrogance. "I beg you, my friendly critics, / Do not set about to procure me an audience."

There is more of the same in "The Condolence" (which strongly echoes Whitman) and in "The Garret," which the poet considered "about the best" of the group he first published in *Poetry*, in April 1913.[18] Literary Bohemianism is rarely so consummately delicate as "Nor has life in it aught better / Than this hour of clear coolness, / the hour of waking together." But it is in "The Garden" that Pound reaches, for the first time, the full height of his powers. He reaches it again and again, in *Lustra*, nor is "The Garden" the best of the poems in the book. But none is better, and it remains, in his ordering of the poems in *Personae*, the first to be encountered.

> Like a skein of loose silk blown against a wall
> She walks by the railing of a path in Kensington Gardens

—and what would Pound have done with this image, earlier?

> Yea, brothers, in the public parkway walketh she,
> And bloweth in the *angst* of her *fainéant* soul
> Like yon piled-up richness out of Lombardy,
> Woven for the likes of such as Guido sang, once, or . . . [19]

"The Garden," on the contrary, is razor clear. We are given exactly what we need to know, and not a jot more. The metaphor is not encumbered with historical baggage; there is no straining to say more than is there to be said. The rhythm follows natural syntax, and though it has the flowing movement of verse it also has many of the linguistic characteristics of prose. "I want it," wrote Pound of twentieth-century poetry, "austere, direct. . . ."[20] He also wrote, with an almost savage trenchancy: "Poetry must be *as well written as prose*. . . . There must be no book words, no periphrases, no inversions. . . . There must be no interjections. No words flying off to nothing. . . . Rhythm MUST have meaning. . . . There must be no clinches, set phrases, stereotyped journalese. The only escape from such is by precision, a result of concentrated attention to what is writing. . . . Objectivity and again objectivity . . . nothing that you couldn't, in some circumstance, in the stress of some emotion, actually say."[21] "The Garden" entirely and quite perfectly fills the bill.

Not all of *Lustra*, to be sure, is perfect. Nor is "The Garden" equal to "Mauberley." But there are other perfections in the book. "The Bath Tub" is in fact far more inventive than it at first seems:

As a bathtub lined with white procelain,
When the hot water gives out or goes tepid,
So is the slow cooling of our chivalrous passion,
O my much praised but-not-altogether-satisfactory lady.

First published in 1913, this shows Pound in command of something very like the simultaneous bite and lyricism of Catullus, who he labelled "the most hard-edged and intense of the Latin poets."[22] Again, he tackles head-on his own prior romanticism: in a letter transmitting the poem to Harriet Monroe, in December 1912, he explained that "The 'Bath Tub' is intended to diagnose the sensation of two people who never having loved each other save in the Tennysonian manner have come upon a well-meaning satiety."[23] The poem is subtly inventive because (1) it makes utterly unselfconscious use of common urban imagery, in a poem dealing with what had always evoked—and in the past had evoked from Pound too—much high-sounding rhetoric, and (2) it manages a kind of verbal coinage without departing from straightforward speech. Indeed, the adjectival "but-not-altogether-satisfactory" works rhythmically as well as lexically, slowing the poem's movement exactly as required; it also helps to underline the maturity suggested, in the previous line, by the phrase "our chivalrous passion." Chivalry had meant something entirely different to Pound not too many years before. The advance is immense—for poetry in English as well as for Pound himself.

The degree of that advance needs underlining. Here is the opening of "The Barberry Bush" by Grace Hazard Conkling, culled from Braithwaite's influential *Anthology of Magazine Verse for 1915*, which included also a review of Mrs. Conkling's first book of poems, *Afternoons of April*, praised as "full of those subtle and delicate fabrics of sunshine and dream which glorifies an April landscape":

Threading the wood, if I might see
A hamadryad leave her tree,
Or Pan with dripping honeycomb
Luring a nymph away from home,
Eager to ask some friendly faun
What way Proserpina had gone.[24]

This smacks a good deal more of the eighteenth than of the twentieth century. The anthology features some better poetry than this, by poets still of reputation, but its pages are largely full of the like of "Spring! / And her hidden bugles up the street," by Louis Untermeyer, and "O, that endlessly earth would stream the heavens / With one music of all-assenting welcome," by Ridgely Torrence (the former Pound's age, the later ten years older). Set against such a background, "The Bath Tub" can be seen as the pioneering and radical poem it in fact was.

There are lighter but essentially similar successes in "The Encounter" and in "Black Slippers: Bellotti," as well as in other poems in the volume. "Tame Cat," on the subject of being "among beautiful women," is masterfully, slyly blunt; "It rests me to converse with beautiful women / . . . The purring of the invisible antennae / Is both stimulating and delightful." The calm social satire of "The Garden"—"And round about there is a rabble / Of the filthy, sturdy, unkillable infants of the very poor. / They shall inherit the earth"—breaks out more passionately, in poems like "Shop Girl":

> For a moment she rested against me
> Like a swallow half blown to the wall,
> And they talk of Swinburne's women,
> And the shepherdess meeting with Guido.
> And the harlots of Baudelaire.

The intense pathos of this little poem is rare in Pound; the conscious turning against the past, when confronted with the urgencies of the present, is also new in the poetry. His conservatism—although in some ways the most radical of men, Pound was surely in some ways a dyed-in-the-wool conservative—emerges in epigrammatic poems like "L'Art, 1910": "Green arsenic smeared on an egg-white cloth, / Crushed strawberries! Come, let us feast our eyes." There are retrogressive poems in *Lustra*, like "Provincia Deserta" and "Dompna Pois de me no'us Cal"; there are half-Whitmanesque satires that do not come off, like "Epilogue" or "Ancora"; there is the eternally delightful but slight "Ancient Music" (which remains vital enough to have made the reputation of a poet less ambitious than Pound); there are Chinese translation-adaptations, anticipatory of *Cathay* (but apparently not drawn from the Fenollosa manuscripts).[25]

But the major accomplishments, in addition to those already touched on, are in two poems of only two lines, in the one case, and of only four words, in the other. "Papyrus" runs in its entirety as follows:

> Spring . . .
> Too long . . .
> Gongula . . .

Although it has been thought to be satirical, and more specifically satirical of the Greek-influenced work of H.D., it has been shown that the poem is in fact based on a Sapphic fragment, and that as a translation is is "at least feasible."[26] But its importance goes beyond translation. It is valuable to emphasize, as later translators have done (in good part under Pound's influence), that poetry transmitted to us only in fragments is irrevocably fragmentary and must not be reduced to a conventional syntactical ordering which it does not contain. "Papyrus" however serves a still more important role in the poetic currents of the English language, underlining in the most graphic way Pound's insistence on "economy of words . . . use no superfluous word," and his praise for "that explicit rendering . . . of the eyewitness."[27] The poets of Braithwaite's *Anthology of Magazine Verse*, a few of them very good poets, had plainly none of them so much as thought of lines so utterly stripped, so perfectly sparse and burnished. It is just one of the many technical innovations which Pound offered to peers and posterity alike; as Dudley Fitts wrote more than forty years ago, "No one who cares anything about poetry, ancient or modern, can afford to disregard Mr. Pound's contribution to it."[28]

"In a Station of the Metro" takes us still further, both in the direction of utterly sparse verse and also in the direction of utilizing the juxtapositions so familiar to us from cinematic usage, and developed in part in response to innovations introduced by artists such as Gaudier-Brzeska. "What have they done for me these vorticist artists? They have awakened my sense of form. . . . The painters realise that what matters is form and color. . . . The image is the poet's pigment."[29] Pound then describes the genesis of "In a Station of the Metro":

> Three years ago in Paris I got out of a 'metro' train at La Concorde, and saw suddenly a beautiful face, and then another and another, and then a beautiful child's face, and then another beautiful woman, and I tried all that day to find words for what this had meant to me, and I could not find any words that seemed to me worthy, or as lovely as that sudden emotion. And that evening, as I went home along the Rue Raynouard, I was still trying and I found, suddenly, the expression. I do not mean that I found words, but there came an equation . . . not in speech, but in little splotches of colour. It was just that—a 'pattern,' or hardly a pattern, if by 'pattern' you mean something with a 'repeat' in it. But it was a word, the beginning, for me, of a language in colour.[30]

He had still not found the poem, but only as he says a "beginning" key to it. After discussing Japanese *hokku* poetry as a " 'one image poem' . . . a form of super-position, that is to say, . . . one idea set on top of another," he records that "I wrote a thirty-line poem, and destroyed it because it was what we call work 'of second intensity'. Six months later I made a poem half that length; a year later I made the following *hokku*-like sentence"—and Pound then transcribes "In a Station of the Metro" as we now know it:[31]

> The apparition of these faces in the crowd;
> Petals on a wet, black bough.

In its original published form Pound inserted extra spacing between phrases, as if to underline and ineluctably emphasize the poem's only partial resemblance to the world of conventional syntax and traditional poetry:

> The apparition   of these faces   in the crowd   :
> Petals   on a wet, black   bough   .

There is something programmatic and over-insistent about the first-published version; the poem is radical enough not to need such mechanical aids. It represents, as also it embodies, a genuinely new way of verbalizing experience, at least in poetry written in English. It was an advance that Pound himself followed up on only in part, but that others have pushed (and are still pushing) in many directions.

"Near Perigord," which opens the section headed in *Personae* (1926), "Poems From Lustra"—in which section are incorporated "Mauberley," to be discussed in this chapter, and "Homage to Sextus Propertius," to be discussed in the chapter that follows—is almost the last of Pound's Provence-influenced poems. Not written in the archaic language of the earlier Provence-inspired work, neither is it composed in the terse lyrical style we have been observing. The largest influence on "Near Periogord" is Browning, but the poem's significance is not that Pound was returning to his earlier themes and approaches; rather, he was starting to grope for something entirely different, hunting an historically connected form that would permit him, he hoped, to collect and ruminate on all the various matters that concerned him. "Near Perigord" may have been started as early as 1913; it first appeared in print in December 1915. Its three sections take seven full pages in *Personae*, and—bluntly—it is distinctly dull. The liveliest portion occurs at the start of section two, almost a hundred lines into the poem:

> End fact. Try fiction. Let us say we see
> En Bertrans, a tower-room at Hautefort,
> Sunset, the ribbon-like road lies, in red cross-light,
> Southward toward Montaignac, and he bends at a table
> Scribbling, swearing between his teeth; by his left hand
> Lie little strips of parchment covered over,
> Scratched and erased with *al* and *ochaisos*.*
> Testing his list of rhymes, a lean man? Bilious?
> With a red straggling beard?
> And the green cat's-eye lifts toward Montaignac.

*al and *ochaisos* = rhyme words in a Provencal poem written by this character in Pound's poem; the Provencal poem had been printed with "Near Perigord"

This is fluent, technically consistent, and well organized, but for all that it is dull, inert. There is no reason for us to care about either the character, who is irretrievably literary and whose various involvements seem thoroughly unimportant, or about his situation or its setting. It is a "ribbon-like road": that is apparently accurate, but of what use to us is the knowledge? In sunset, surely, there is "red cross-light": Pound is describing the scene realistically, but to what purpose? Suppose it were night; suppose he did not mention the light or its source. Would there be any difference? This is an early form of the technique that Pound was to develop, as he was already starting to develop it, for use in his *Cantos*: the *Cantos* too began with Browning-derived poetry, and their first versions are much like "Near Perigord." Fuller discussion needs to wait for chapter six, when we reach the *Cantos*. It is enough to note that it is typical of Pound to have reached a peak—and almost immediately to begin abandoning it for something new, assuming axiomatically that anything new was better than, because different from, anything old.

"Villanelle: the Psychological Hour," first published in the same issue of *Poetry* that carried "Near Perigord," neither is, nor was intended to be, a formal villanelle. "I wanted the effect of a recurrence of theme and meant 'Villanelle' to mean generally the feel of the villanelle form in a modern subject."[32] The poem is distinctly reminiscent of Eliot's "Prufrock," which Pound had long since read (and submitted on Eliot's behalf); it lacks "Prufrock" 's intensity, leaning perhaps too much toward the sort of thing that Henry James did at much greater length, and with greater depth, in many of his stories: "Two friends: a breath of the forest . . . / Friends? Are people less friends / because one has just, at last, found them?" There is a certain amount of this pleasant, careful, but essentially dithering verse in most of the poems that precede "Mauberley" in this section of *Personae*. "Pagani's, November 8," may have been faintly scandalous once; it is no more than slight today, quietly charming but no more than that. "To a Friend Writing on Cabaret Dancers" is interesting largely because it shows that "Near Perigord" is neither a sport nor an accident. Pound is reaching determinedly for some uniting methodology, some poetic approach that will permit him not only to escape his medievalist and classicist past (though "Homage to Quintus Septimius Florentis Christianus" is a collection of six translations from the *Greek Anthology*), but enable him to make use of his own present, his own day-to-day experiences. Again, connecting past and present is the key element in this search, and fuller discussion must be postponed until we reach the *Cantos* themselves.

"Langue d'Oc," a sequence of four translations from the Provencal, was originally published under the title "Homage à la Langue d'Oc." In a long letter to his old teacher at the University of Pennsylvania, Felix E. Schelling, Pound wrote a few years later that "There is, however, a beauty in the troubadour work which I have tried to convey. I have failed almost without exception." As to the archaic language, once again resorted to, he argues rather elliptically that "the Latin is really 'modern.' We are just getting back to a Roman state of civilization, or in reach of it; whereas the Provencal feeling is archaic, we are ages away from it. (Whether I have managed to convey this or not I can't say; but it is the reason for the archaic dialect.)"[33] Perhaps: Pound is notoriously polite to epistolary critics, often agreeing—for the moment, and possibly forgetting other views and positions—with their most basic objections to particular work. It seems to me equally doubtful that "In LANGUE D'OC . . . the archaisms are functional: Pound wanted to create an idiom that would contrast sharply with the colloquial freedom of HOMAGE TO SEXTUS PROPERTIUS."[34] Pound wanted to do what he wanted to do because he wanted to do it. "Pound preferred intuition to taking pains,"[35] as Alexander neatly puts it. I have mentioned Pound's praise of Henry James, oddly, as a "hater of tyranny." He adds, in that long and fascinating 1918 essay: "The outbursts in *The Tragic Muse*, the whole of *The Turn of the Screw*, human liberty, personal liberty, the rights of the individual against all sorts of intangible bondage!" And then he goes on, in a long footnote: "What he fights is 'influence', the impinging of family pressure, the impinging of one personality on another; all of them in highest degree damn'd, loathsome and detestable. Respect for the peripheries of the individual may be, however, a discovery of our generation." Returning to his text, he exlaims: "The passion of it, the continual passion of it in this man who, fools said, didn't 'feel'. I have never yet found a man of emotion against whom idiots didn't raise this cry."[36] Nor does Pound stop hammering away at this point. "There was emotional greatness in Henry James' hatred of turanny," he proclaims a page later. James was "susceptible . . . to the tone and tonality of persons as perhaps no other author in all literture. . . . He emerged into his greatness . . . by reason of his hatred of personal intimate tyrannies working at close range. . . . The hatred of tyrannies was as great a motive as any we can ascribe to Galileo or Leonardo or to any other great figure, to any other mythic Prometheus; for this driving force we may well overlook personal foibles," and so on.[37] It is the same thing he finds to praise in Swinburne: "The passion not merely for political, but also for personal, liberty is the bedrock of Swinburne's writing. . . . A magnificent passion for liberty—a passion dead as mutton in most of his contemporaries."[38]

These seem to me fundamental attitudes, of enormous importance in trying to arrive at some more or less final understanding of Pound and of his poetry. I cannot explain the etiology of such obviously passionately held beliefs; I do not think that anyone can explain them, lacking much fuller understanding of the dynamics of Pound's childhood and family life. We may never have that fuller understanding—but the attitudes are clearly linked to much that otherwise will continue to seem inexplicable about Pound.

"Moeurs Contemporaines" (Contemporary Manners/Ways) was published, originally, together with "Homage à la Langue d'Oc," and it has been argued that the two sequences are meant to be read together, as a contrasting of medieval and modern manners and morals.[39] This seems to me after-the-fact canonization of a passing fancy, even perhaps a pure piece of happenstance (or an accident of editorial decision: as Pound wrote to the poet Marianne Moore, in 1919, "it would be criminal for me to refuse £10/10. . . . It don't matter in the least what appears or does not appear in that magazine."[40]). The eight poems, and "Cantico del Sole" which immediately follows them (it had appeared in the same magazine two months earlier), are genial satires, nicely sharpened, and sufficiently concrete and particular for the reader both to comprehend and to savor their well-honed jabs. Nor is this a truly unusual side of Pound: he certainly could and did refer to "Masefield's diarrhoea [and] Abercrombie's dessicated feces," and to an anonymous rumor-monger as "a bloody and louse-eaten liar," and to "the sacks of pus which got control of Brit. pubctn. [publication] in or about 1912."[41] But Ford Madox Ford was not being hyperbolic when he assured Pound that "your heart is golden,"[42] nor was William Carlos Williams exaggerating when he recalled Pound as "the liveliest, most intelligent and unexplainable thing I'd ever seen, and the most fun. . . . And he had, at bottom, an inexhaustible patience, an infinite depth of human imagination and sympathy."[43]

> And she said:
>> "You remember Mr. Lowell,
> "He was your ambassador here?"
> And I said: "That was before I arrived."
> And she said:
>> "He stomped into my bedroom. . . .
> (By that time she had got on to Browning.)
> ". . . stomped into my bedroom. . . .
> "And said: 'Do I,
> " 'I ask you, Do I
> " 'Care too much for society dinners?'
> "And I wouldn't say that he didn't.
> "Shelley used to live in this house."
>
> She was a very old lady,
> I never saw her again.

"Pound is a master of the indulgent sneer," wrote Maxwell Bodenheim, referring to "Moeurs Contemporaines" as a whole. "The result may be unfair to the person criticized, but it is effective."[44] This seems to me to sadly distort the geniality of Pound's satire. The penultimate poem in the sequence, number 7, begins "They will come no more, / The old men with beautiful manners." Where is the sneer? Poem number 6 contains only four English lines: "After years of continence / he hurled himself into a sea of six women. / Now, quenched as the brand of

Meleager, / he lies by the poluphloisboious [loud-resounding]
sea-coast." Poem number 2, which is I think the emotional
center of the entire sequence, is both a taut and a moving
analysis:

> At sixteen she was a potential celebrity
> With a distaste for caresses.
> She now writes to me from a convent;
> Her life is obscure and troubled;
> Her second husband will not divorce her;
> Her mind is, as ever, uncultivated,
> And no issue presents itself.
> She does not desire her children,
> Or any more children.
> Her ambition is vague and indefinite,
> She will neither stay in, nor come out.

Pound was always both wary and saddened by the indecisive-
ness of others, male and female alike. His first communication
to the young poet Mary Barnard, for example, asks bluntly
"Age? Intentions? Intention? How MUCH intention? I mean how
hard and for how long are you willing to work at it? . . . Nice gal,
likely to marry and give up writing or what Oh?"[45] The last
paragraph of his impassioned, profoundly moving letter to Felix
E. Schelling, April 1934, demands poignantly why his old
teacher refuses to act, even when "you are too respected and
respectable for it to be any real risk. They can't fire you *now*.
Why the hell don't you have a bit of real fun before you get
tucked under? / / Damn it all, I never did dislike you."[46] These
are the forces, and the inner voices, that should be heard under
the deft satire of "Moeurs Contemporaines." There is tolerance
and wonderment even in the nastiest of the lot, number 4:

> At the age of 27
> Its home mail is still opened by its maternal parent
> And its office mail may be opened by its parent of the
>   opposite gender.
> It is an officer,
> > and a gentleman,
> > > and an architect.

So too there is bemused realism in the exposure of America's continued provincialism, in number II and in "Cantico del Sole" (Canticle/Song of the Sun). "The thought of what America would be like / If the Classics had a wide circulation / Troubles my sleep." This is, we must keep in mind, the man who wrote to the editor who printed "Cantico del Sole" the year before she printed the poem,

> The one use of a man's knowing the classics is to prevent him from imitating the false classics. . . . The classics, "ancient and modern," are precisely the acids to gnaw through the thongs and bulls-hides with which we are tied by our schoolmasters.
>
> They are the antiseptics. They are almost the only antiseptics against the contagious imbecility of mankind.
>
> I can conceive of an intelligence strong enough to exist without them, but I can not recall having met an incarnation of such intelligence.[47]

In his *ABC of Reading* Pound defines his terms: "A classic is classic not because it conforms to certain structural rules, or fits certain definitions (of which its author had quite probably never heard). It is classic because of a certain eternal and irrepressible freshness."[48] And the fierce integrity with which Pound defended these standards, by which he himself strove always to live his life as a writer (an integrity which is displayed on almost every page of his *Letters*), makes his "antiseptic" notion a vital one. After refusing to contribute to an anthology being put together by William Rose Benet, who as assistant editor of *The Saturday Review of Literature* was in Pound's view "pouring poison into or onto the enfeebled or adolescent Amurkn mind; or at any rate doing yr. . . . damdest to preserve mildew," Pound was offered a larger fee to contribute, that being why the editor thought he had refused. "I appreciate your kindness in cabling [Pound was in Italy] but I am afraid I shall have to be even more explicit in my answer." He then details his principled objections and concludes, quite magnificently, "How the deuce do you expect me to swallow all that for the sake of a small sum of money?"[49] Or writing to the ambitious, talented, but second-rate and backbiting Amy Lowell, he asked with a humor (and a seriousness) not unlike "Moeurs Contemporaines," "once more, pas de bile [no bad temper], before it is too late, do you wish to repent and be saved? . . . It ain't, no dearie, it AIN'T good for the nerves. The eye of the needle is narrow."[50]

Which brings us to "Hugh Selwyn Mauberley (Life and Contacts)," "so distinctly a farewell to London," Pound notes in early editions of *Personae*, "that the reader who chooses to regard this [book] as an exclusively American edition may as well omit it." It is indeed a farewell, but it is a great deal more than simply London—which in fact he was leaving, first for Paris and then for his more or less permanent home in Italy—to which he is bidding goodbye. Froula is crisply accurate: "it is a farewell to the aestheticism which had played a large part in his poetry up to this point, and, at the same time, an ironic and bitter indictment of modern society, in which what we now refer to as 'Kitsch' has displaced serious art."[51] "Mauberley" is an eighteen-poem sequence, occupying eighteen full pages in *Personae*: I can do no more than outline its major themes and accomplishment.[52]

Much of "Mauberley" is retrospective. Faced with a changed world, in good part because of World War One and its physical and psychological destruction, Pound reconsiders what his own life and art have been about, finding (in the concluding line of the first poem) that "the case presents / No adjunct to the Muses' diadem." In this "Ode pour l'élection de son sepulchre" (Ode for the selection / choice of his [own] tomb), Pound is unsparing of his earlier self, which had been "wrong from the start." "Out of key with his time," he says flatly, "He strove to resuscitate the dead art / Of poetry; to maintain 'the sublime' / In the old sense." There is certainly irony here; the danger would be to permit a confusion of irony with either lack of seriousness, on the one hand, or despair or self-pity, on the other. "Mauberley" is as serious as poetry can be; it is angry, it is passionate, but it is neither self-pitying nor is it indicative of any sort of surrender.[53] Explanations are not excuses: not really "wrong from the start," he explains, "seeing he had been born / In a half savage country, out of date." The reference to Capaneus, of the Seven Against Thebes, who had been struck down by Zeus for boasting that not even the lightning of the king of the gods could harm him, is too condensed; on closer acquaintance with Pound's work one finds that in his 1910 *Spirit of Romance* he had endorsed Dante's notion that Capaneus should remain "unrelenting in his defiance of the supreme power,"[54] and that in Canto LXXIX, one of the Pisan Cantos, Capaneus reoccurs once again.[55] But overly condensed or not, the reference indicates the kind of tough-mindedness that Pound advocates. Capaneus died unrepentant, according to Dante, and in a poem about himself Pound clearly means an identification to occur to the reader. "His true Penelope was Flaubert"—was, and still is, though in fishing "by obstinate isles" he has not had much of a catch. Very well: he is someone "unaffected by 'the march of events' "—that is, not a man of or dominated by headlines and "current affairs." He will pass "from men's memory," and into a new endeavor in a new place. "Bent resolutely on wringing lilies from the acorn," and failing, he will try to construct something both new and different, as well as stronger than mere "lilies." "Tenny rate, whooz down-hearted," as he concludes a long letter some years later to Harriet Monroe.[56] More to the point, "I desire to go on with my long poem," the *Cantos*, and having gotten "Mauberley" off his hands that is of course exactly what he did.[57]

The second poem in the sequence declares bitingly (and there is none of the gentleness of "Moeurs Contemporaines" anywhere in "Mauberley"), that "The age demanded an image / Of its accelerated grimace / . . . Better mendacities / Than the classics in paraphrase!" The third poem broadens the indictment: Christianity and the material civilization that it developed have substituted, Pound says, for "the mousseline [muslin] of Cos"—a singularly fine cloth woven on the Greek island of Cos—only "the tea-rose tea-gown etc." In matters religious "Dionysus,./ Phallic and ambrosial"—that is, sexual and intoxicating—has been replaced by the "macerations" (the wearing or wasting away) of Christ's body into wafers consumed by the faithful. This is one of the most compressed of the poems in the sequence, and I do not think its poetry equals the best of the other poems. But the broadening of the indictment against modern civilization is thematically important; without it poems four and five, directly attacking World War One, would be distinctly decreased in significance.

> Died some, pro patria,
>> non "dulce" non "et decor"*
> walked eye-deep in hell
> believing in old men's lies

The intensity of Pound's condemnation, toward the end of poem number four, almost sabotages the poetry; he rescues it with the final two lines:

> Daring as never before, wastage as never before.
> Young blood and high blood,
> fair cheeks, and fine bodies;
>
> fortitude as never before
>
> frankness as never before,
> disillusions as never told in the old days,
> hysterias, trench confessions,
> laughter out of dead bellies.

Much of this passage hovers on the edge of sentimentality— "young blood . . . high blood, / fair cheeks . . . fine bodies." But the passionate denunciation, and the return to poetic specificity and clarity at the end, saves things. It is in this poem, too, that we first hear not only of "old men's lies" but of "usury age-old and age-thick," concepts and words the *Cantos* will make great play on. Poem five, which I want to quote in its entirety, is in a sense a further condensation of poem four—and very much its superior as poetry:

> There died a myriad,
> And of the best, among them,
> For an old bitch gone in the teeth,
> For a botched civilization,

---

*Pro patria / non "dulce" non "et decor" = for their country / not "sweetly" not "properly"

Charm, smiling at the good mouth,
Quick eyes gone under earth's lid,

For two gross of broken statues,
For a few thousand battered books.

This is one of the finest antiwar poems ever written: it, and not the sincere but clumsy efforts of Wilfred Owen, Isaac Rosenberg, Siegfried Sassoon, et al, is the true poetic heritage of World War One. And though Pound's "true Penelope" is still Flaubert, can it be doubted after poem five that both his denunciation and his retrospective self-denunciation are deadly serious? His earlier life had been dedicated precisely to those "few thousand battered books." Now he will try to pass by "the elegance of Circe's hair," and focus instead on the "old bitch gone in the teeth," try as best he can make some repairs in the "botched civilization."

The next four poems, appropriately, focus on aspects of the corruption in art which matches, and which supports, the corruption in civilization as a whole. "Yeux Glauques" (Grey Eyes) deals with the treatment of pre-Raphaelite art and artists in Victorian England. Gladstone was a British prime minister; Robert Buchanan had attacked the pre-Raphaelites in an essay, "The Fleshly School of Poetry." The woman with the "faun's head" serving as a model is probably Elizabeth Siddal, who married Rossetti and, after a difficult life, committed suicide. Fitzgerald's *Rubaiyat* was accidentally discovered, on a remainder table, by Rossetti; "poor Jenny" refers to a Rossetti poem about a tired prostitute; appropriately, a "macquero" is a pimp. Cophetua refers to a legendary African king, a womanhater until he met, married, and found immense happiness with a beggar maid "all in grey" (perhaps that being the reason Cophetua is in the poem). These are today somewhat obscure references; they were much less obscure in 1920, to a poet who had been living in late Victorian and early modern England. Neither this nor poem seven, " 'Sienna Mi Fe'; Disfecimi Maremma' " ("Sienna Gave Me Birth, Maremma Death," words spoken by La Pia in Dante's *Purgatorio*; Rossetti made a painting on this subject), seem nearly so passionate, on the surface, as the war poems which precede them. But the apparently calm surface is deceptive. "Foetid Buchanan," in "Yeux Glauques" (poem six), and the deftly savage phrase, "the pure mind / Arose toward Newman as the whiskey warmed," from poem seven, show that Pound is deeply involved. The poems are less powerful, certainly, but that is not inappropriate, considering both their subject matters and their place in the overall sequence of "Mauberley."

Poem eight marks another first, namely the appearance of Pound's anti-Semitism. Brennbaum may, from the physical description in the poem, be modelled on Max Beerbohm (who was not in fact Jewish, though many so thought him), but the details are unimportant and the poem distinctly inferior. "Mr. Nixon," which seems to be based on the highly successful and extremely prosperous Arnold Bennett, is in need of neither annotation nor commentary: it is exactly what it appears to be, an attack on a "commercial" writer, an artist who has almost by definition sold out. The poetry is not of high intensity, though the thematic material is totally appropriate.

Poem ten, probably written about Ford Madox Ford, is considerably more complex than "Mr. Nixon." In part it is a combination of some of the Chinese poems that Pound had been working on (particularly in the celebration of a lonely writer shut away in a broken down cottage) with the witty quatrains of Théophile Gautier (who plainly influenced much of the writing throughout "Mauberley"). The portrait of fervent (and presumably honest) literary "sophistications and contentions" leaking "through [the] thatch of the roof" marks an obvious contrast with the "cream gilded cabin of [the] steam yacht" belonging to Mr. Nixon. The final lines condense Pound's firm, even passionate affirmation into two lovely images of "succulent cooking" (Ford was in fact a first-rate chef) and a door, forever unlocked (to those who deserve entry) but with "a creaking latch." The same condensation is missing from poem eleven, a rather ineffectual attack on middle class women and their sexual limitations. Ealing is a middle class London suburb; the Milesian Tales of ancient Greece, which have not survived, were supposed to be fabulously erotic and licentious. But the poetry is stillborn, here. Poem twelve is somewhat better: its portrait of the typical fashionable literary salon in the London of those days is suitably negative. But there is remarkably little bite in the satire (and rather too many words). "The sale of half-hose has / Long since superseded the cultivation / of Pierian roses," alludes to a Sapphic line (Pieria was the spot near Mount Olympus where the Muses were worshipped); this is pleasantly but hardly impressively satiric.

"Envoi," which concludes part one of "Mauberley," is a difficult poem to fully account for. On the one hand, it is both a rewriting of Edmund Waller's seventeenth-century lyric, "Go, Lovely Rose" (which had been set to music by Henry Lawes), and a reassertion of exactly that cult of beauty, " 'the sublime' in the old sense," that the first poem in "Mauberley" confesses to have been "wrong from the start." On the other hand, coming in the position in "Mauberley" where Pound has placed it, it can also be seen as a self-conscious, almost self-parodying representation of why the cult of beauty was "wrong from the start," the lyric tradition in which Waller and Lawes had worked being quite dead. To attempt to resurrect the dead, accordingly, is to oblige oneself to speak in dead voices—an obviously poor idea. "In the duplicity of its motives," argues Froula, "the 'Envoi' is a brilliantly contrived exit from the double-bind Pound represents in *Mauberley*."[58] I am not convinced: it does not seem to me possible for poetry to actually accomplish that much, on that many levels, at the same time. It may well be that Pound was thinking in such terms; it may also be that he had not thought out his position to anything like this sort of clarity. In either case, "Envoi" is to my mind ineffectual and out of place. It might have made sense in *A Lume Spento*; I do not think it makes much sense here.

The remaining poems, added after the main part of "Mauberley" had been written, are all of lesser intensity, and they do not add much to the thematic presentation. The first of them, "Mauberley," indicates that Pound had ideas of creating an alter ego of a sort, named Hugh Selwyn Mauberley, by means of whom notions relevant to the subject matter of the sequence could be better delineated. How closely Pound identified Mauberley with E. P., in the "Ode" which constitutes the first poem of the sequence, is both undeterminable and, in the final analysis, not terribly important. "I'm no more Mauberley than Eliot is Prufrock," Pound declared sensibly.[59] But Pound has not fully controlled his material in these final poems. They are full of dry abstractions, hints that are never elaborated or given poetic flesh. "Colourless / Pier Francesca, / Pisanello lacking the skill / To forge Achaia" is, I am afraid, what might be called push-button poetry, relying on things totally external to itself to convey what poetry ought to convey. I do not mean that allusions and references are intrinsically signs of poetic weakness, but simply that, in these poems, Pound does not translate his allusions into anything more than allusions. They lie on the page and, as poetry, do little or nothing. It is a problem about which much more will need to be said when we come to the *Cantos*.

Somewhat flawed (especially in its concluding portions), "Mauberley" remains a sequence containing much power and passion. Its principal themes, again, are two: a disavowal of Pound's prior literary beliefs and practices, and an attack on the society which could no longer accept or even tolerate such beliefs and practices—a society whose corruption and decadence is further indicated both by the mere fact of World War One and by the tawdry cheapness of its most prominent, most successful literary practitioners (and their hangers on). Mr. Nixon has a yacht; "the stylist" is forced to live under a "sagging roof." Pound's condemnation, in the epigraph to the second poem in the last group, is expressed through a pseudonym, and is further disguised by being written in French—but then, in Pound's view, anyone worth communicating with would not regard French (or a good many other languages) as an obstacle of any sort. "What do they know of love," he demands, "and what are they able to understand of it? If they do not undertand poetry, if they do not feel music, what can they understand of that passion in comparison with which a rose is gross (crude) and the scent of violets is a thunderbolt?" "So far as I am personally concerned," he had written to Harriet Monroe almost eight years earlier, "the public can go to the devil."[60] "Once and for all dammmm the audience. They eat us. We do not eat them," he told the same correspondent in 1914. And in 1917 he wrote in a magazine editorial, "There is no misanthropy in a thorough contempt for the mob. There is no respect for mankind save in respect for detached individuals."[61] But though he had not retracted those views, he had expressed them in these ways before "Mauberley," before turning away into the *Cantos*, before trying somehow (he did not really know how) to help reconstruct the broken world in which he suddenly realized he had been living all along. It was a true turning point, a deep transition. But it was also a beginning from which he had no idea how to proceed, or where he might be led. Passionate though he was, his uncertainties—for they were many—had profound consequences for both his later life and his later poetry.

4 Europe and the Orient Pound as a Translator

Pound had much of the training of a scholar in comparative literature, including an M.A. and much of the work toward a Ph.D. But as he says forthrightly in the preface to his 1910 *Spirit of Romance*, "This book is not a philological work. Only by courtesy can it be said to be a study in comparative literature. I am interested in poetry. . . . My criticism has consisted in selection [of original texts and their translations] rather than in presentation of opinion." He notes, too, that "I would in all seriousness plead for a greater levity, a more befitting levity, in our study of the arts."[1] In chapter five, on Pound as a critic of matters literary and social, we will pursue the critical perspectives from which he operated—which were clearly not those of a comparatist or indeed of any sort of scholar. The two primary characteristics of scholarship are fidelity (to texts or facts or both) and fullness of inquiry. Pound saw texts and facts alike as building blocks intended for his use, and in the preface to *Spirit of Romance* he concedes that "there is no attempt at historical completeness." He then refers, jestingly, to a German *Grundriss* (Outline) which though exceedingly scholarly ("Tedescan," Pound quips) and "21,000 folio pages" long, is also incomplete. "To this admirable work I cheerfully recommend anyone who has a passion for completeness."[2]

As a translator, Pound worked from a dozen different languages, some of which he knew well and most of which he knew to some degree; there were some languages from which he worked only at secondhand. It is a formidable list: Italian, French, Spanish, Provencal, Latin and Greek (the languages he knew best); German and Old English, which he knew reasonably well; Chinese, of which he had a smattering; and Japanese, Egyptian, and Hindi, which he knew not at all. His translations fall into three rough classifications, only the second and third of which will concern us here: (1) trots (not intended to be read as poetry but as guides to the original), (2) poems (including imitations) from languages Pound could control, and (3) poems (including imitations) from languages Pound could not control. The translations which come under the first category, more or less literal trots, are for the most part those Pound made for *The Spirit of Romance*; over and over again he introduces them by a prefatory "Roughly," or notes that "it would take several translations and some comment to exhaust the beauty of the original"[3]—or else simply gives up and renders poetry into straightforward prose. He occasionally apologizes for the fact that his original "is infinitely more beautiful than the bare sense in English" and frequently adds that his reader must learn the language of the original because, for example, "Certain of Dante's supremacies are comprehensible only to such as know Italian."[4] At one point he fairly cries out: "The following translation is appaling in its crudity."[5] This is not the Ezra Pound whose translations have given joy to thousands of readers, and bellyaches to thousands of scholars, but the Ezra Pound who, especially early in his career, was still in part a scholar *manqué*. We do not need to be concerned with this side of Pound in this chapter.

But Ezra Pound the translator of poetry into poetry is by no means a consistent, unitary figure. I have said that he is essentially an appropriative translator: that is, he goes to an original because it has something he wants. There can be no question that he admires, and frequently passionately admires, the beauties of the texts he chooses for translation; there has seldom been anyone, poet or critic or scholar, whose relish of poetic beauty remained all his life so keen. In "How I Began," written in 1913, where he declares his intention to "know more about poetry than any man living," he goes on to explain this decision to know the dynamic content from the shell . . . what part of poetry was "indestructible," what part could *not be lost* by translation . . . what effects were attainable in *one* language only and were utterly incapable of being translated.

In this search I learned more or less of nine foreign languages. . . . Of course, no amount of scholarship will help a man write poetry, it may even be regarded as a great burden and hindrance, but it does help him to destroy a certain percentage of his failures. It keeps him discontented with mediocrity.[6]

Appropriation is not programmatic; it does not dictate exactly what can be obtained in any particular translation, nor does it require that the same things be obtained (or sought) in each and every line of a particular translation. Appropriation is basically as indifferent to consistency as it is, in the final analysis, to the integrity of the text being translated; what emerges from the spigot, what is carried over into English, is everything, and the means by which that ultimate goal may be attained are entirely flexible. "I do not know that strict logic will cover all of the matter," Pound wrote in 1919, "or that I can formulate anything beyond a belief that we test a translation by the feel, and particularly by the feel of being in contact with the force of a great original."[7] As to things in the original which may get in the translator's way, "obscurities *not inherent in* the matter, obscurities due not to the thing but to the wording, are a botch, and are *not* worth preserving in a translation."[8] In plainer terms, anything that troubles you can be omitted, so long as you do not think it central; the mere words of the original are in no way binding. "The artist seeks out the luminous detail and presents it."[9] And if the artist is Ezra Pound, much of the time that luminous detail will glow indeed. "Mr. Pound," wrote Ford Madox Ford, "has a genius for words that no one—not excluding Shakespeare in England or Heine in Germany—has ever in modern times much surpassed."[10] The statement is accurate, as is Donald Carne-Ross's assertion that Pound, if anyone, is "the

creator of modern verse translation . . . his translations . . . are
. . . a body of work that for range and originality is unparalleled
in English poetry."[11]

It is Pound's practice, accordingly, that must be looked to
for any degree of understanding (and appreciation) of his various methodologies. And since for him it all pretty much began
with Latin, and among Latin poets with Catullus, let us begin
exactly there:

> Salve, nec minimo puella naso
> nec bello pede nec nigris ocellis
> nec longis digitis nec ore sicco
> nec sane nimis elegante lingua,
> decoctoris amica Formiani.
> ten Provincia narrat esse bellam?
> tecum Lesbia nostra comparatur?
> o saeclum insapiens et infacetum!

This is Catullus: 43. A kind of trot, with key words in alternative
form, would look like this:

> Greetings, not the smallest female nose
> nor pretty foot nor black eyes
> nor long fingers nor mouth dry
> nor particularly sensitive tasteful tongue
> of the bankrupt (old rake) Formianus the girlfriend.
> You the Provinces tell us are pretty (beautiful)?
> You with our Lesbia are compared?
> Oh age unwise (unsensible) and un-clever (un-witty, un-
> brilliant)!

"The colloquialism of Catullus," writes the classical scholar
Kenneth Quinn, "is, of course, well recognized by scholars,
though it is seldom adequately represented by Catullus' many
translators in recent years. . . . If we are to get the right feeling
for Catullus, we must grasp [the] way in which his language
(despite its colloquial raciness), by a subtle infiltration of the
unobtrusively archaic, the unusual and even the exotic, assumes
the evident tone, the solemnity almost, that serious poetry
requires."[12] Catullus's language being crucial, Louis Zukofsky

(in many ways a poetic disciple of Pound's) has translated poem 43 with obviously excessive attention to the Latin language of the original:

> Salvé, next, poor little nosey,
> next below, padded foot, no grace of black eyes,
> next longish digitals, next aura, sick o
> not synonymous with an elegant tongue,
> decocted mistress of a weak Formiani.
> In the Province they think—now rate—you a belle?
> Take you for Lesbia, compare you to her?
> O cycles of fashion, yet the facts hate them![13]

Except for a sudden flash of normal English in the penultimate line, this is hardly translation at all, as also it is hardly English. Pound knew better, in theory as well as in practice: "We have long since fallen under the blight of the Miltonic or noise tradition, to a stilted dialect in translating the classics, a dialect which imitates the idiom of the ancients rather than seeking their meaning. . . . [Milton] tried to turn English into Latin; to use an uninflected language as if it were an inflected one, neglecting the genius of English, distorting its fibrous manner, making schoolboy translations of Latin phrases. . . . Copies of Greek and Latin clause structure and phrase structure . . . have removed the classics from us."[14] Here is Pound's translation:

To Formianus' Young Lady Friend

after Valerius Catullus

All Hail; young lady with a nose
    by no means too small,
With a foot unbeautiful,
    and with eyes that are not black,
With fingers that are not long, and with a mouth undry,
And with a tongue by no means too elegant,
You are the friend of Formianus, the vendor of cosmetics,
And they call you beautiful in the provinces,
And you are even compared to Lesbia.

O most unfortunate age!

This is not academic translation, but with one exception it is clearly a rendering of the Latin. In line five of the original Pound has managed to transform *decoctoris*, "a ruined man, a bankrupt," into something drawn from *decoris*, "charm, ornament": there is no "vendor of cosmetics" in the original. The final line, too, is as much summary or paraphrase as it is exact translation. But the grace, concision, and force of Catullus has in fact been carried over—as a few comparative verse translations will make clear:

How do you do, girl with the outsize nose,
Colourless eyes, stub fingers, ugly toes,
Coarse conversation and lips none too dry,
Friend of the bankrupt man from Formiae.
Are you the lady whom Cisalpine Gaul
Ranks with my Lesbia and dares to call
Beautiful? O provincial generation—
No taste, no culture, no imagination!

(James Michie)

Girl with the not inconsiderable nose,
Sizable feet and eyes not exactly jet-black,
With fingers scarcely long and mouth which can
    hardly be called dry,
And a tongue you are in the habit of sticking out,
You who go to bed with the Formian bankrupt:
You are reported in the Province to be beautiful?
My Lesbia is compared with you?
What an uncultivated age we live in!

(C. H. Sisson)

Listen, girl: your nose is not too small and
your foot somehow lacks shapeliness, your eyes
are not so bright, your fingers though they should be

are neither long nor graceful, nor can your lips
(mouth dripping) be kissed for love, nor is your
   speech soft music.
And this girl is the lady friend
of that debauched citizen Mamurra.
They say that you are lovely (rumours from the
   provinces)
comparing you with Lesbia.

The times are bad
and this an ignorant generation.

                              (Horace Gregory)

O elegant whore!
      with the remarkably long nose
unshapely feet
      lack lustre eyes
fat fingers
      wet mouth
and language not of the choicest,
you are I believe the mistress
of the hell-rake Formianus.

And the Province calls you beautiful;
they set you up beside my Lesbia.
O generation witless and uncouth!

                              (Peter Whigham)

There are many more versions one could cite; I believe this will
be sufficient. What the competing translations prove is that Ford
Madox Ford was right: Pound "has a genius for words."
Pound's taste becomes "luminous" indeed when compared to
the rhyming flatness of Michie, the awkward upperclass En-
glishness of Sisson, the uncontrolled sprawling wordiness of
Gregory, and the imaginative but hopelessly unlyrical
Whigham. Pound *knew* that Catullus *sang*: "I doubt if Catullus is

inferior to Sappho,"[15] he declared roundly, "Catullus has the intensity."[16] None of Pound's minor freedoms with literal meaning, nor even his one howler, can alter or explain away the fact that he, alone of the translators of this poem, has truly gotten to the heart of it and has successfully transferred as much of that central poetic reality over into English as is possible. This fact makes it difficult to comprehend the sometimes frenzied hostility of his academic critics. William Arrowsmith (as fine a classicist as our time has seen) and Roger Shattuck comment: "Among many scholars it is still suspected that 'free' translation is something first invented, with characteristic perversity, by Ezra Pound, who is, in fact, nothing more than the latest exponent of a millenial tradition."[17] He may be in fact the latest exponent, but he is also, on the record, at the very head of that millenial tradition. "No major poet between Pope and Ezra Pound devoted himself centrally to translation," notes Carne-Ross;[18] no poet ever devoted himself more successfully or more importantly to translation.

"Pound has put Cathay back on the map, and made it live again in all its glory. . . . [His] versions are incomparable," notes Hugh Gordon Porteus of the translations contained in *Cathay* (1915).[19] And since his Chinese renderings make Pound, in T. S. Eliot's words, "the inventor of Chinese poetry for our time"[20]— perhaps a bit extravagant but not too far from the sober truth— let us turn to Pound's "The River-Merchant's Wife: A Letter." This is by Rihaku, he tells us, not knowing in his "total ignorance of the Chinese language" that this is the Japanese transcription of Li Bai (also anglicized as Li Po or Li Bo).[21] It is a thirty-line poem, which makes comparisons a bit clumsy, but Pound's translation is so extraordinarily beautiful that any awkwardness of presentation is well worth laboring through. Wai-lim Yip, who gives the title as "The Song of Ch'ang-kan," has translated the poem literally, "to show the line-unit [in Chinese] and general format" and strictly "for the sake of comparison":[22]

> My hair barely covered my forehead.
> I played in front of the gate, plucking flowers,
> You came riding on a bamboo-horse
> And around the bed we played with green plums.

  5   We were then living in Ch'ang-kan.
      Two small people, no hate or suspicion.
      At fourteen, I became your wife.
      I seldom laughed, being bashful.
      I lowered my head toward the dark wall.
 10   Called to, a thousand times, I never looked back.
      At fifteen, I began to perk up.
      We wished to stay together like dust and ash.
      If you have the faith of Wei-sheng,*
      Why do I have to climb up the waiting tower?
 15   At sixteen, you went on a long journey
      By the Yen-yü rocks at Ch'ü-t'ang
      The unpassable rapids in the fifth month
      When monkeys cried against the sky.
      Before the door your footprints
 20   Are all moss-grown
      Moss too deep to sweep away.
      Falling leaves: autumn winds are early.
      In the eighth month, butterflies come
      In pairs over the grass in the West Garden.
 25   These smite my heart.
      I sit down worrying and youth passes away.
      When eventually you would come down from the
            Three Gorges
      Please let me know ahead of time.
      I will meet you, no matter how far,
 30   Even all the way to Long Wind Sand.

This is a lexical translation but not in any sense a poetic one (Yip
has published poetry in English and knows the difference).
Pound's version has only 29 lines, for he conflates lines 25 and
26:

          While my hair was still cut straight across my
                forehead
          I played about the front gate, pulling flowers.

---

*Wei-sheng = man who died under a bridge, waiting for a girl who did not
come: his faith was so intense that he stayed—and drowned—expecting
her to keep her promise

You came by on bamboo stilts, playing horse,
You walked about my seat, playing with blue plums.
5   And we went on living in the village of Chokan:
Two small people, without dislike or suspicion.

At fourteen I married My Lord you.
I never laughed, being bashful.
Lowering my head, I looked at the wall.
10   Called to, a thousand times, I never looked back.
At fifteen I stopped scowling.
I desired my dust to be mingled with yours
For ever and for ever and for ever.
Why should I climb the look out?

15   At sixteen you departed,
You went into far Ku-to-yen, by the river of swirling
    eddies,
And you have been gone five months.
The monkeys make sorrowful noise overhead.

You dragged your feet when you went out.
20   By the gate now, the moss is grown, the different
    mosses,
Too deep to clear them away!
The leaves fall early this autumn in wind.
The paired butterflies are already yellow with August
Over the grass in the West garden;
25   They hurt me. I grow older.
If you are coming down through the narrows of the
    river Kiang,
Please let me know beforehand,
And I will come out to meet you
                As far as Cho-fu-Sa.

These are clearly versions of the same poem; just as clearly there
are variations in detail. Some of these are condensations, as in
lines 13, 14, and 16, where Pound turns three allusions familiar
to literate Chinese into more generalized expressions of emotion. "Pound, determined to abandon annotations, has always
tried to get around allusions without deviating from the essential poem," notes Yip, adding that as "between annotations and

poetry, one is compelled to make a choice."[23] Line one is another sort of alteration: Pound clarifies what a Chinese reader would know without further explanation, and his added detail is accurate. Line four is badly mangled, both as translation from the Chinese and translation into English. That is, the sense of the line has been mangled, and "You walked about my seat" has vague but unfortunate associations that Pound surely did not intend. (Such errors may be caused by his long absence from both his home country and, later on, from any country where his native language was spoken. How else, for example, explain the slightly ludicrous legend on his personal notepaper, "for the public convenience"?) Line seventeen is simply wrong as translation, though it makes sense enough in Pound's poem-version. Lines 19 and 20 are rather embroidered, but not overly so; use of the Japanese transcription of the original Chinese, Cho-fu-Sa, rather than either the Chinese or a translation thereof, is of no intrinsic importance linguistically—and adds a great deal to the poem.[24]

The singular virtues of the translation may not be fully clear until we look briefly at competing versions. "You, my lover, on a bamboo horse," write Witter Bynner and Kiang Kang-Hu, "Came trotting in circles and throwing green plums." This is not only erroneous but ludicrous. The same translators render lines 11 through 14: "But at fifteen *I straightened my brows* and laughed, / Learning that no dust could ever seal our love, / That *even unto death* I would await you *by my post* / And would *never lose heart* in the tower of silent watching" (italics added). The combination of ripe awkwardness and flowering cliche is poetically deadly. Arthur Cooper, a more recent translator, does not do the entire poem quite so awfully as he does the first four lines:

> I with my hair fringed on my forehead,
> Breaking blossom, was romping outside:
>
> And you rode up on your bamboo steed,
> Round garden beds we juggled green plums.

It is hard to keep a straight face, reading lines so inept. Cooper's scholarly knowledge of Chinese and its literature exceeds

Pound's by far, but that does him very little good when it comes to poetry. Robert Payne does the poem more acceptably, though still without Pound's magical touch: "My hair could hardly cover my forehead; / I was plucking flowers near the door. / Then you came riding a bamboo horse / And threw green plums near my bed." (All the same, that last line suggests, risibly, some wild primitive fertility rite.)

"In a loose sense, all the poems in *Cathay* are, to some extent, Poundian," writes Yip, "because the cuts and turns of the mind in the original poems are either overemphasized or modified according to his own peculiar gestures of expression."[25] To the extent that this is true, and meaningful, it says little more than that all translation is partial and to a degree both fallible and subjective.[26] But Yip penetrates a good deal further into Pound's special gifts as a translator:

> Although Pound has been sharply limited by his igno-
> rance of Chinese . . . he possesses a sense of rightness,
> an intuitive apprehension in poetic organization or, to
> borrow a term from Eliot, 'the creative eye' which we
> should not begrudge giving due credit. For even within
> the limits of free improvisation and paraphrase . . . he
> sometimes tends to come closer in sensibility to the
> original than a literal translation might. . . . Strangely
> enough, Pound has occasionally (by what he calls
> 'divine accident'?)penetrated below a faulty crib to the
> original and come out right.[27]

There are of course times, in *Cathay* and elsewhere, when Pound does not come out right, places where even reasonably solid linguistic knowledge and enormously well-schooled literary sense do not save him. His version of the Old English "The Seafarer" can be seen, as I have said, in such terms, though for that poem I would prefer to simply acknowledge that the translation process is, for Pound, appropriative rather than in the more usual scholarly sense transmissive. But what do we do with translations like the eight-line "Anadyomene" ("she who rises" out of the sea, Venus, Aphrodite)?[28]

As it might have been from under a green tin coffin-lid,
A woman's head with brown over-oiled hair
Rises out of a theater box, slow and stupid
With ravages in rather poor repair.

Then ups the fat grey neck and bulgy shoulder-blades,
The shortish back going out and in
And the fat, in clumsy slabs under the skin,
Seems ready to emerge without further aids.

This is said to be "From Rimbaud," and Rimbaud not only often sounds exactly like this, and strikes attitudes of this sort, but he is one of those poets of whom it is almost impossible to make a good translation. Pound has not preserved anything even approximating the likely French meter, but he has managed some deft rhyming. And then one looks at the French original, entitled "Vénus Anadyomène," and discovers, first, that this is only the first eight lines of a sonnet. Pound has cropped poems before; so too have other translators. It is not ultimately a very serious matter, though acknowledging such cropping does make things clearer. But the French original reveals something else, too; something a good deal more serious—Pound has set the poem in a theater, with the fat and ugly woman's head rising "out of a theater box." It may be intrinsically plausible, but it is definitely not what Rimbaud's French says: "Comme d'un cercueil vert en fer blanc, une tête / De femme à cheveux bruns fortement pommadés / D'une vieille baignoire émerge." ("As from/out of a green tin/zinc coffin, a woman's head with brown hair strongly/heavily pommaded emerges from an old bathtub.") It is not a coffin-lid from which the woman's head rises, but a coffin-like object, and that object is not a theater box but a bathtub. The key word is *baignoire*, which can in fact mean either theater box or bathtub, but which the rest of the poem—and indeed some of the poem that Pound has actually translated—clearly indicates can here mean only bathtub. In line 7, for example, where Pound speaks only of "the fat, in clumsy slabs under the skin," Rimbaud writes of "les rondeurs des reins," the "rotundity/fullness of the buttocks/loins." And the final three lines, gross but vividly clear, are: "Les reins portent deux mots gravés: CLARA VENUS; / —Et tout ce corps remue et tend sa large croupe / Belle hideusement d'un ulcère à l'anus." In plain prose, "There are two words engraved (tatooed?) on the buttocks: CLARA VENUS;—and that whole body moves and sticks out/ protrudes its large rump, hideously beautiful with an ulcer on/at the anus." It would be hard to imagine even Rimbaud setting such a description in a theater box. The whole second part of the poem, and as I have said a part that Pound has translated, makes it clear that *baignoire* cannot mean theater box. Pound surely knew that the word meant bathtub as well; but even if he did not, he should have been alerted by the remainder of the poem. Plainly, he knew something was wrong, or at least was aware of something which led him to mangle lines 7 and 8. In the French the lines read: "Puis les rondeurs des reins semblent prendre l'essor; / La graisse sous la peau paraît en feuilles plates." ("Then the rotundity/fullness (the curves) of the buttocks seem to soar; the fat/lard under the skin looks like/appears to be/resembles flat flakes/slabs.") Pound's final line, "Seems ready to emerge without further aids," is nowhere to be found, neither in the octave nor in the sestet of the French sonnet. Pound wants this eighth and in his poem final line to rhyme with "blades"; "aids" gives him that rhyme. The interpolated line also enables him to end his version, as the eighth line of the French original would not. But what is Pound really up to? Has he, as he plainly had in "The Seafarer," some larger conception of the poem which requires him to both crop and recast it as he has done? It is perhaps possible, but it does not seem likely. It is much more likely, unfortunately, that Pound first made his basic mistake, taking *baignoire* to mean theater box rather than bathtub, and only then, as if in unconscious (or partly conscious) defense of his own view, rewrote lines 7 and 8 and eliminated the rest of the poem.

This explanation is the likely one for a number of reasons, all of them deeply important for any overall understanding of Pound as a translator. In 1912, when "The Seafarer" had only recently been published, Pound recorded that "I have been much questioned . . . how much of this translation is mine and how much the original." Let me, before reproducing Pound's astonishing answer, repeat what I have written in chapter three of Pound's "Seafarer": "What Pound does not do—does not try to do—is translate in the usual sense of that word. That is, the verbal meaning, as opposed to the verbal music, is of minimal importance to him. When it becomes necessary to slight, or even to discard lexical significance, in order to produce the aural effects he is after, he does not hesitate." I have given more than enough examples in chapter three; there are many more that could be listed. This description of Pound's operating procedure in "The Seafarer" is not intended to be hostile; it is simply descriptive, conclusively factual. Pound's assertion, accordingly, is at the very least astonishing: " 'The Seafarer' was as nearly literal, I think, as any translation can be."[29] What are we to make of this assertion? Hugh Kenner's earliest work on Pound would have us believe that "The whole key to Pound, the basis of his *Cantos*, his music, his economics, and everything else, is [his] concern for exact definition."[30] But can any man so profoundly gifted in the use of the English language possibly mean what he says of his "Seafarer" translation? Are we to assume, perhaps, that the qualifying clause—"as nearly literal . . .*as any translation can be*" (emphasis added)—is what saves it from being, on its face, sheer nonsense?

I think not. What we must assume, in my judgment, is that Pound is almost never to be taken literally—including those times when he uses the word "literal." All things were pliable, flexible, and relative to Pound, and verbal things most of all. His "attention," Kenner writes in an excellent essay, "tended to fix on the constelled words in ancient texts, not on their syntactic connexions." To this quite accurate appraisal, which can be (and has been) tracked through virtually all his translations of no matter what variety and from no matter what language, Kenner adds the following totally persuasive analysis:

> It is tenable that he saw diction rather than syntax because not having learned declensions accurately he could not follow the syntax. This is very likely often true, but does not of itself explain why a man who was never lazy, and had an appetite for detail, and was

75

passionately interested in old poems, did not feel an incentive to perfect his grammatical knowledge. That he was impatient with people who possessed such knowledge is not an explanation but something else to explain. What did he know that they didn't? Which means, since a man will not willingly pore over what is opaque to him, what was he responding to when he read Greek? To rhythms and diction, *nutriment for his purposes*" (emphasis added).[31]

Pound was definitely not lazy, and he emphatically had—as the *Cantos* prove—a large appetite for detail. There is not the slightest doubt that he loved "old poems." It is not that Pound knew something those with grammatical knowledge do not know, but rather that he was only interested in what interested him, and saw only what he wanted (chose?) to see. "Pound's academic respect for the literal sense of a poem," observes Ruthven a bit sadly, "is overwhelmed by his poetic interest in what he can make of it by treating it as the starting point for something else." He adds: "Having tried and failed to systemize his methods I leave the reader with . . . the general warning that Pound never hesitated to be literal, free, or fanciful whenever he felt so inclined." And he concludes with the caution that "As a general rule we can learn to distrust Pound whenever he tries to justify his mistranslations as part of 'the new method in literary scholarship,' "[32] that being indeed what Pound had claimed for his "Seafarer" version.

There is another element at work, as well, and one which I mention not to denigrate but only to help explain Pound. Although he was capable of acting with manners equal to the best, he was frequently rude—abrupt, nasty, apparently totally indifferent to the feelings of others. His correspondence, as I have already noted, shows him sometimes extravagantly deferential, sometimes bitterly abusive. He interpreted others' actions, and their literary work, in the same way. "He had become so engrossed in the satirical aspect of [James Joyce's] *Ulysses* that he took it for granted [Joyce's] new book would be similar. 'J. J. launched on another work', he wrote to his father in August [1923], 'Calculated to take the hide off a few more sons of bitches.' "[33] The new work was *Finnegan's Wake,* and Pound's description was wildly off target. His biographer records that, on the one hand, Pound was so passionate about taking care of the cats in Italy that "large numbers wait him every night at a certain street corner knowing that his pocket is full of meat bones or chicken bones."[34] And on the other hand, his megalomania could and did lead him to decide "that the Christian Era had ended at midnight on 29–30 October, 1921: the world was now living in the first year of a new pagan age called the Pound Era."[35] Similarly there was on the one hand his fabled generosity, and on the other his paranoia: "In 1930 P[ound] was able to state," he wrote of himself in the third person, "that NO american publisher had *ever* accepted a book on his recommendation! No am. univ. or cultural institution had ever invited him to lecture (this despite his double qualification as author and man of learning) nor had he ever been invited to serve on any jury of awards to art, music or literature, not had any fellowship to a writer ever been made on his recommendation."[36] Both the language and the substance are considerably exaggerated. Pound had always within him the poles of thought and feeling, just as, in all likelihood, he also had always within him the seeds of what seemed even to his friends madness, long before his post-World War Two incarceration in the psychiatric ward of a Washington D.C. hospital. "In Paris in 1934 Joyce had asked [Hemingway] to come along to dinner with Pound because he [Joyce] was convinced that Pound was 'mad' and was 'genuinely frightened of him'. Throughout dinner, Hemingway said"—and it should be emphasized that none of Pound's friends stood by him more valiantly and with more loyalty than did Hemingway—"Pound spoke 'very erratically.' "[37]

The consequences of all this for Pound's criticism will be examined briefly in the next chapter. Here, it needs to be emphasized that it takes nothing whatever from Pound's immense positive accomplishments as a translator to say that he did not always operate at his own highest level in that (or in any other) field. When he first botched, and then insisted on perpetuating, even adding to, his botch of the Rimbaud poem examined earlier, he plainly exhibited his worst side. It would be as foolish to deny that side as it would be to deny that, in other translations he would do the same thing ad libitum, as and when and if he pleased. In his book-length study of the "Homage to Sextus Propertius"—a study so sensitive and thorough that further commentary would be otiose—J. P. Sullivan notes that Pound "sometimes let himself be led by the suggestions of the Latin text into mere word play and phrase-mongering." He also shows how Pound labelled the "Homage" a translation, then denied that it was a translation, at the same time claiming that "I can so snugly fit into the words of Propertius almost thirty pages with nothing that isn't S[extus] P[ropertius], or with no distortion of his phrases that isn't justifiable by some other phrase of his elsewhere."[38]

Pound did what he did as a translator, and was what he was as man, and translator, and poet. To recognize him is perhaps to begin to understand him; it is emphatically not to blame him for not being or doing something quite different.

5 A Prose Proteus
Pound as a Critic, Literary and Social

Pound is not thought of as a systematic critic; certainly, in the usual sense of "systematic," he can easily be mistaken for the most casual and scattered commentator ever to exist. But closer acquaintance with, and more careful understanding of, his prose works, especially in the literary field, reveals a high order of consistency, centered in a number of primary stances:

1. Literature, as an affair of morality as well as entertainment, is an intensely serious matter
2. Those who are concerned with and respond to literature both wish and need to be instructed, particularly about literatures other than those written in their native languages
3. Repetition is essential to communication, especially in matters ideational (as contrasted to matters emotional)

Pound's critical prose is by no means confined to literature, however, though a selection of his literary criticism fills a closely printed volume of close to five hundred pages.[1] He has also written instructional prose, *How to Read*, *ABC of Reading*, and a 379 page *Guide to Kulchur*.[2] And he has written, though largely in more fugitive style, on economics and politics: I will principally refer to the collection of his World War Two radio speeches broadcast from Italy, now published as *"Ezra Pound Speaking"*.

Categorization is inevitably an imposition from the outside, and at best an approximation: in his criticism as in his other work Pound overlaps himself freely and even wilfully. These three main divisions of criticism—literary, instructional, and economic and political—are neither Pound's own categorizations nor compartmentalizations he would have been likely to accept. I do not propose to try holding him to classifications quite alien to his whole way of thinking, but only to use these three divisions as a general guide to discussion. Pound's perception of himself, from the start, included a significant messianic element, a prophetic urgency which endured all through the productive years of his life. Stock records that, at age seventy-two, his health poor and his writing days largely behind him, "Pound decided that he would like to build at the summit [of a Brunnenburg mountain known as 'Mut'] a marble temple with three columns; he was driven to a nearby quarry and the project was found to be within reach, but nothing more was done about it."[3] It was much like the radical university he had proposed to establish much earlier, or some of the magazines he had proposed to found: there were always more projects, more books, more everything than could possibly have been handled by any one man, even a man so energetic as Pound. He sparked ideas and proposals—intensely and seriously, but a bit wantonly—as a candle burns or water flows downhill. It is the nature of the man; it spreads all through his critical writing, as it does through his poetry and his translations; and his readers, whether sympathetic or not, must in any event recognize with whom they are dealing. As Ford Madox Ford wrote to Harriet Monroe in 1913, when Pound tried to resign as foreign editor of *Poetry* and have Ford take his place, "I think it would really be much better for you to go on with Ezra and put up with his artistic irritations; because he was really sending you jolly good stuff. That is the main thing to be considered, isn't it?"[4]

LITERARY CRITICISM

Formal literary criticism—or criticism as formal as Pound cared to make it—must necessarily be our focus. But since so much of Pound's most trenchant literary comment comes to him on the wing, in letters or suddenly as he discusses something else and wants to make a literary point, let me begin this discussion with, first, a two-line satirical poem from *Lustra,* and then with Pound's August 1917 letter to John Quinn (his and many other artists' patron), spiritedly defending and explaining the true purport of the poem. It is impossible to recapture Pound's quicksilver conversation, in which so much of his literary influence was expressed. But we have his letters, and we are lucky to have them: they are an indispensable text for twentieth-century poetry in English.

The New Cake of Soap

Lo, how it gleams and glistens in the sun
Like the cheek of a Chesterton.

Dear John Quinn: . . . I am worried by your cable received this A.M. re the two lines on Chesterton. Do what you like about them. Only they are part of my position, i.e., that one should name names in satire. And Chesterton is like a vile scum on the pond. The multitude of his mumblings cannot be killed by multitude but only by a sharp thrust (even that won't do it, but it purges one's soul).

All his slop—it is really modern catholicism to a great extent, the *never* taking a hedge straight, the mumbo-jumbo of superstition dodging behind clumsy fun and paradox.

If it were a question of cruelty to a weak man I shouldn't, of course, have printed it. But Chesterton *is* so much the mob, so much the multitude. It is not as if he weren't a symbol for all the mob's hatred of all art that aspires above mediocrity.

I feel very differently about Belloc, who once wanted to do the real thing, and for a long time, at least, had moments of bitterness (I think) that he had taken the journalistic turning. Still, he has left "Avril" and his translation of Bédier's *Tristan*.

Chesterton has always taken the stand that the real thing isn't worth doing. (Perhaps this is a slight exaggeration???? Complex of my own vanity??) My feeling is, perhaps, heightened by a feeling that I should probably like G. K. C. personally if I ever met him. Still, I believe he creates a milieu in which art is impossible. He and his kind. . . . On the other hand, the lines are contemptuous, and contempt may not be a very formidable weapon.[5]

This is as close as we are likely to get to the cut-and-thrust of Poundian talk; it is an appropriate introductory text in a discussion of his literary criticism, which is similarly rapier-like, passionate, and yet in the end often calm and fair as well. Seventeen years after the letter partially reproduced above was written, Chesterton wrote a very complimentary review of Pound's prose: "There are two things about Mr. Pound that I like: he is very learned, which I am not; and he has furious likes and dislikes, which I have but should hesitate to state so furiously." There was as Pound had half predicted a rapprochement; about a year after Chesterton's review appeared Pound was, in a letter written to him, linking them as soldiers on the same side in a common war.[6] And two years later, Chesterton having died, Pound attacked "the respectable . . . illustrious punks and messers, fakes like Shaw, stew like Wells, nickle cash-register Bennett. All degrading the values." But referring to his earlier views and pronoucements he at once added: "Chesterton meaning also slosh at least then and to me."[7] It is not simply that he was loyal, though he distinctly was, but also that he was always willing, even eager, to admit what he later saw as a mistake. As in everything else, Pound's literary views are not to be taken literally, or as set in concrete.

His *Literary Essays,* edited in 1954 by T. S. Eliot, and some sections of his *Selected Prose,* edited in 1973 by William Cookson, offer the basic texts of his literary criticism. There also is relevant material in *The Spirit of Romance,* which after three quarters of a century remains a useful, readable appreciation of medieval and early Renaissance literature in Europe. "I believe that in the study of literature," he wrote in the last-named 1910 volume, "one should read texts, not commentaries."[8] It remains one of the basic reasons for reading what Pound has to say about other writers. Even in 1910, Pound had achieved the energized, pulsing prose that distinguishes his work from virtually all other literary criticism: "Dante's god is ineffable divinity. Milton's god is a fussy old man with a hobby."[9] "For sheer dreariness one reads Henry James, not the *Inferno*."[10] (One of the views he significantly recanted.) "Camoen's type of mind [is] the mind of a man who has enthusiasm enough to write an epic in ten books without once pausing for any sort of philosophical reflection. He is the Rubens of verse."[11]

Another of Pound's bon mots from his early treatise on medieval and early Renaissance writers could almost serve as an epigraph to any discussion of his literary criticism: "The single line is, it is true, an insufficient test of a man's art, but is a perfect test of his natural vigor, and of his poetic nature."[12] As he is in his own poetry, Pound as a critic is usually relentlessly specific—a characteristic of such great poet-critics as John Dryden, T. S. Eliot, and W. H. Auden, but in Pound raised to unusual heights. In writing of Charles Vildrac, for example, a French poet three years his senior, Pound takes us in detail through the poem being examined, quoting, commenting, highlighting. "After the first words, when [the character in the narrative] had come into the light and sat down, between this man and his companion, both surprised and 'empressés'—however you want to translate it. Eager. / / Il s'aperçut qu'on lui ménageait. / / (Another untranslatable word. I suppose we might say, 'He felt that they were beating about the bush'. . . . Then there was a 'detente' (literally a discharge as of a pistol). . . . I have been told that this is sentiment and therefore damned. I am not concerned with that argument. . . . The point is that M. Vildrac has told a short story in verse with about one fifth of the words that a good writer of short stories would have needed."[13] Pound is focussed, he knows what he is looking for and knows exactly when he has (or thinks he has) found it. And he looks at the text, often very closely indeed: he does not try (or tries not to try) to rewrite what another man has set down on paper. If he does not find what he wants or likes in a poem, novel, or book, he does not write criticism about it: this is a fundamental restraint that more formal, academic critics might well emulate. In a 1917 essay he asserts that Thomas Beddoes

"[1803–1849] is perhaps more 'Elizabethan' than any so modern poet, that is, if by being 'Elizabethan' we mean using an extensive and Elizabethan vocabulary full of odd and spectacular phrases." He cites examples, calling the first "magnificent rhetoric," but then, introducing a different example, finds himself obliged to admit: "Very well, says the opponent in my head, but this is 'Romanticism', there is nothing Elizabethan about it." Pound then produces yet another passage—and concedes the validity of the objection: "At any rate this strophe is lyric."[14] Pound *listens* to that "opponent in my head": in spite of any and all critical deficiencies, he remains a deeply honest man, as critic as well as poet. It is a deeply redemptive trait.

Of the three sections into which Eliot has divided *Literary Essays*, parts one and three, "The Art of Poetry" and "Contemporaries," each occupy roughly twenty percent of the volume; the second and much the largest section, "The Tradition," occupies about sixty percent. It is a fitting division: from the Troubadors to Swinburne and Remy de Gourmont, Pound's attention was always focussed above all else on those writers who constituted and shaped, what he defined in 1913 as "a beauty which we preserve." And he immediately adds, "and not a set of fetters to bind us."[15] It is the terms of this definition of "The Tradition" (the title of the essay) that are distinctive. T. S. Eliot is at least as centrally concerned with tradition, but early and late Eliot defines it very differently. "The historical sense," he wrote in a famous 1917 formulation, "compels a man to write not merely with his own generation in his bones, but with a feeling that the whole of the literature of Europe from Homer and within it the whole of the literature of his own country has a simultaneous existence *and composes a simultaneous order*" (emphasis added).[16] Pound is after "a beauty which we preserve"; Eliot seeks, as always, "order." "It is impossible to fence off *literary* criticism from criticism on other grounds," Eliot affirmed in 1961, "moral, religious and social judgments cannot be wholly excluded."[17] It is impossible to imagine Pound having written that sentence, though he did write on religious subjects from time to time (and also wrote poems celebrating Jesus Christ, such as "Ballad of the Goodly Fere," and more than one poem in celebration of Christmas). "My criticism has this in common with that of Ezra Pound," Eliot explained in 1956, "that its merits and its limitations can be fully appreciated only when it is considered in relation to the poetry I have written myself." And then Eliot adds: "In Pound's criticism there is a more didactic motive: the reader he had in mind, I think, was primarily the young poet whose style was still unformed."[18] But if Pound is truly "more didactic," it is only in Eliot's rather limited application of the term. Pound's god, as D. H. Lawrence correctly said, was beauty; to this god he strove to convert everyone he could reach, and he could plainly best reach the young, "whose style was still unformed." Pound's evangelism in his literary essays is strictly in service to this one mighty god, while Eliot's allegiance and evangelism belonged only to the Christian god.

"A return to origins," Pound writes in "The Tradition," "invigorates because it is a return to nature and reason. The man who returns to origins does so because he wishes to behave in the eternally sensible manner. That is to say, *naturally, reasonably, intuitively*" (emphasis added.[19] If this sounds essentially Greek and pagan, it is; and it is not accidental that, even at age seventy-two, he still thought in terms of building temples. But most of his critical work dealt not with the Greeks, but with the French and Italians. Of the fourteen essays Eliot has grouped under the overall rubric "The Tradition" in the second and bulkiest part of Pound's *Literary Essays*, only two deal with the Greeks and Romans, and even then only at second hand, through one essay on Elizabethan classicists and another on early translators of Homer. There are however nine essays in which French and Italian poets are centrally considered. (Which leaves three essays for, respectively, George Crabbe, Swinburne, and Henry James.) One can quarrel with the inclusion of this essay and the exclusion of that—as Pound himself did, Eliot tells us. But the "representative choice" that Eliot aimed for seems to me to have been achieved, and the weight thus placed on Dante, Guido Cavalcanti, Arnaut Daniel, on Jules Laforgue and Remy de Gourmont, seems just. "Our poetry and our prose have suffered incalculably whenever we have cut ourselves off from the French," Pound wrote in 1917.[20] "If a man knew Villon and the *Sea-farer* and Dante . . . he would, I think, never be able to be content with a sort of pretentious and decorated verse which receives praise from those who have been instructed to like it," he wrote three years earlier, "or with a certain sort of formal verbalism which is supposed to be good writing by those who have never read any French prose." He adds: "It is possible that only Cavalcanti and Leopardi can lift rhetoric into the realm of poetry."[21] Why deny one's own origins? Pound would have denied that he was doing any such thing. "No American poetry is of any use for the palette," he explained. "A care for American letters does not consist in breeding a contentment with what has been produced, but in setting a standard for ambition. . . . I dare say it is, in this century, inexplicable how or why a man should try to hold up a standard of excellence to which he himself can not constantly attain. . . . [But] a sound poetic training is nothing more than the science of being discontented."[22]

"The history of an art is the history of masterwork, not of failures, or of mediocrity," Pound had said in 1910.[23] That was why, when he steeped himself in Dante and in the Provencal Troubador poets, he experienced contentedness, and found beauty, and proclaimed his discoveries as loud and far as he knew how. "Dante's precision . . . comes from the attempt to reproduce exactly the thing which has been clearly seen."[24] Precision meant the search for and the unearthing of beauty; underneath the principle lay the practice, the actuality of the exact and therefore beautiful line. "The *Paradiso* holds one by its pervading sense of beauty; even so, lines 79–80 of Canto XXIII stand out from the surrounding text. . . . One might indefinitely continue the praise of Dante's excellence of technique and his splendors of detail; but beneath these individual and separate delights is the great sub-surge of his truth and his sincerity: his work is that sort of art which is a key to the deeper understanding of nature and the beauty of the world and of the spirit."[25] That last phrase, "and of the spirit," is both untypical and unconsummated; even in this early work Pound immediately declares that "for the praise of that part of his worth which is fibre rather than surface, my mind is not yet ripe, nor is my pen skilled."[26] If he believed that in 1910, by 1914 (at least) he knew himself better: "One might learn from Dante himself all that one could learn from Arnaut [Daniel]: precision of statement, particularization."[27] But even in 1910, in praising a somewhat lesser singer, Cavalcanti, Pound knew better where his truth really lay: "These are no sonnets for an idle hour. It is only when the emotions illumine the perceptive powers that we see the reality. It is in the light born of this double current that we look upon the face of the mystery unveiled. I have lived with these sonnets and ballate daily month in and month out, and have been daily drawn deeper into them and daily into contemplation of thing that are not of an hour."[28] The language is faintly musty; there is Edwardian rhetoric afoot. But it is not spiritual matters that Pound is drawn deeply into the contemplation of. "In the art of Daniel and Cavalcanti," he wrote in the clearer prose of 1917, "I have seen that precision which I miss in the Victorians, that explicit rendering, be it of external nature, or of emotion. Their testimony is of the eyewitness, their symptoms are first hand."[29]

Indeed, so distinctly is Pound's concern one of uncovering beauty and the methods by which it is attained—which means technique, and not something of the spirit: "let the [poetic] candidate fill his mind with the finest cadences he can discover, preferably in a foreign language," as he put it in 1913[30]—that much of his critical attention, in dealing with Daniel, Cavalcanti, and Dante, is devoted to verse forms, prosody, and the like. Indeed, his essay, "The Tradition," concludes with a series of prosodic pronoucements: "The movement of poetry is limited only by the nature of syllables and of articulate sound. . . . Space forbids a complete treatise on melody at this point, and forbids equally a complete treatise on all the sorts of verse. . . . And such treatises . . . are for the most part useless, as no man can learn much of these things save by first-hand untrammeled, unprejudiced examination of the finest examples of all these sorts of verse, of the finest strophes and of the finest rhyme-schemes."[31] "The forms of [Troubador] poetry are highly artificial," he writes in 1913, but rather than apologize for artificiality he actively embraces it: "and as artifice they have still for the serious craftsman an interest, less indeed than they had for

Dante, but by no means inconsiderable."[32] The long essay on Arnaut Daniel is focussed on "the best fashioner of songs in the Provencal, as Dante said of him . . . , trying the speech in new fashions, and bringing new words into writing, and making new blendings of words."[33] For example, we hear, and are given examples of, "clear sounds and opaque sounds, such as in *Sols sui*, an opaque sound like Swinburne at his best; and in *Doutz brais* and in *L'aura amara* a clear sound, with staccato; and of heavy beats and of running and light beats, as very heavy in *Can chai la Fueilla*."[34] Pound sarcastically comments at the start of the essay's second part that "The twenty-three students of Provencal and the seven people seriously interested in the technic and aesthetic of verse may communicate with me in person."[35] "I have found out what I have found out," he explains in his "Cavalcanti," "by concentration on the text, and not by reading commentators, and I strongly suspect that is the road the next man [to study these matters] will have to follow." Accordingly a good deal of his commentary reads like this:

> The canzone was to poets of this period what the fugue was to musicians in Bach's time. . . . The strophe is here seen to consist of four parts, the second lobe equal to the first as required by the rules of the canzone; and the fourth happening to equal the third, which is not required by the rules. . . . Each strophe is articulated by 14 terminal and 12 inner rhyme sounds, which means that 52 out of every 154 syllables are bound into pattern. The strophe reverses the proportions of the sonnet, as the short lobes precede the longer. . . . As to the use of canzoni in English, whether for composition or in translation: it is not that there aren't rhymes in English; or enough rhymes or even enough two-syllable rhymes, but that the English two-syllable rhymes are of the wrong timbre and weight.[36]

A poet is apt to find this meat-and-drink, and fascinating; the average reader of more usual literary criticism is apt to be bewildered and quickly bored. I do not mean that there is no more than this in "Cavalcanti": there is in fact a good deal more than this, and much of general literary interest. "It takes six or eight years to get educated in one's art, and another ten to get rid of that education," Pound notes along the way.[37] But within two paragraphs he is back to the differences between the sonnet form in Italian and English, the necessity for "singing" in verse, for keeping unbroken "the single uninterrupted flow of sylla-bles."[38] Again, Pound's literary criticism must as Eliot correctly noted be constantly referred back to Pound's other writing, or it cannot be properly understood. Pound is a supreme technician: it is the most natural thing in the world for him to focus on technical matters in his criticism. "I do not believe that a man's critical activities interrupt his creative activities in the least," Pound asserted. "As to writing criticism, it is not a question of effort. It is merely a question of whether or no a man writes down what he thinks."[39] "Pound's ideas are responsible for most of the good writing in verse in the 20th century," says the poet Louis Simpson. "Above all, he gave us a language to write in. . . . Pound made poets look at things as they were, and say what they truly saw and felt. . . . He revitalized poetry as Wordsworth had a hundred years before. . . . But he never had a center of his own."[40] The final statement may not be wholly true, but there is surely a significant element of truth in it—and for Pound the poet-technician to be obsessed with the techniques of poetry simply makes good sense. "To say that any kind of criticism has its limitations," T. S. Eliot wrote in introducing Pound's *Literary Essays*. "is not to belittle it, but to contribute towards its definition and understanding. The limitation of Pound's kind is in its concentration upon the craft of letters, and of poetry especially. . . . On the one hand, this very limitation gives him a wider range. . . . But when we want to understand what a foreign literature means, or meant, to the people to whom it belongs, when we want to acquaint ourselves with the spirit of a whole civilisation through the whole of its literature, we must go elsewhere. . . . You can't ask everything of every-body."[41]

INSTRUCTIONAL MANUALS

There are three primary texts, *How to Read* (1931), *ABC of Reading* (1934), described by its postwar publishers as "an extension of the argument followed by the author in his essay on *How to Read*," and (probably) *Guide to Kulchur* (1938). I include the last-named under this rubric, rather than under the social and political writing, because on balance there seems to be more similarity to *How to Read* and *ABC of Reading* than to, say, "*Ezra Pound Speaking*." It does not make a great deal of difference for my purposes, for I shall have very little to say about *Guide to Kulchur*, a rag-bag of a book if ever there was one. Stock was not writing specifically of this book, but of Pound's entire orientation in the 1930s and the 1940s, when he wrote:

> Intellectually he was now at the mercy of the pseudo-system of thought, which, with his rare zeal, he had manufactured out of Fenellosa and bits and pieces of information and learning. He had convinced himself that he possessed a method which enabled him to recognize the meaning of things without having to submit to any discipline or go through any process of abstract thought. In practice it meant no more than that he picked up information from old books, newspapers, monetary reform pamphlets, etc., and meditated upon them, using, within the limits of his nineteenth-century heritage, the method of abstraction which he claimed to despise.[42]

Pound asserts, for example, that "I suggest that finer and future critics of art will be able to tell from the quality of a painting the degree of tolerance or intolerance of usury extant in the age and milieu that produced it."[43] "The code of [Thomas] Hardy's time, and Hardy's plots all imply monetary pressure."[44] "Babbitt is the state of mind . . . which can see without boiling, a circumjacence, that tolerates Mellon and Mellonism, the filth of american govt. through the reigns of Wilson, Harding, Coolidge and the supremely uncultivated, uneduated gross Hoover, the England that swelters through the same period and the France of that period, and every man who has held high office in these countries without LOATHING the concessions made to foetor and without lifting hand against them, and against the ignorance wherein such mental squalor is possible."[45] There is good sense, at times; there is even humor, as when Pound wonders (in a section entitled "Maxims of Prudence"), "Has Eliot or have I wasted the greater number of hours, he by attending to fools and/or humouring them, and I by alienating imbeciles suddenly?"[46] But *Guide to Kulchur* is not a guide to anything; it offers little enlightenment on any subject, including the one here at issue.[47]

How to Read is an exceedingly short work, truthfully an essay printed on a small page, in a large type, and heavily leaded. Pound saw it as a book of "demands";[48] for all his paranoia and his frequent yelps of disapproval and dismay, he also saw it as yet another "endeavour to communicate with a blockheaded epoch."[49] "To tranquilize the low-brow reader," Pound explains, "let me say at once that I do not wish to muddle him by making him read more books, but to allow him to read fewer with greater result."[50] It is an accurate formulation of his goal. All the same, pages five through eleven are essentially a rambling, autobiographical complaint against the unreceptivity of the British establishment to his ideas (and to ideas generally). Then he gets to the point: "We could . . . apply to the study of literature a little of the common sense that we currently apply to physics or to biology . . . if the instructor would select his specimens from works that contain [genuine] discoveries," of which there are "in each age one or two men of genius [who] find something, and express it."[51] Why bother, and why in particular bother with books, especially literary books? Because "it appears to me quite tenable that the function of literature as a generalized prize-worthy force is precisely that it does incite humanity to continue living; that it eases the mind of strain, and feeds it, I mean definitely as a *nutrition of impulse*." Here is beauty worship with a vengeance—and Pound is well aware of it. "This idea may worry lovers of order," he adds immediately. But literature, he says with some heat, is not meant to propagate *any* ideas. "It has to do," instead, "with the clarity and vigour of 'any and every' thought and opinion. It has to do with maintaining the very cleanliness of the tools, the health of the very matter of thought itself."[52] I have said, in chapter one, that Pound saw literature as an imperative moral force, and that he saw Italy "destroyed by rhetoric." There are sixteen years between the assertion about Italy's destruction and the emphasis, in *How to Read*, on "maintaining the very cleanliness of the tools." But the statements are the same, and proceed from the same, unchanging concern with what, in another context, he called "the simplicity of *adequate* speech."[53] These are cardinal matters to Pound; he never changed his view of them. "The great writers need no debunking. The pap is not in them, and doesn't need to be squeezed out. They do not lend themselves to imperial and sentimental exploitation. . . . [Great writing] maintains the precision and clarity of thought, not merely for the benefit of a few dilettantes and 'lovers of literature,' but maintains the health of thought outside literary circles and in non-literary existence, in general individual and communal life. . . . [Indeed,] one 'moves' the reader only by clarity. In depicting the motions of the 'human heart' the durability of the writing depends on the exactitude."[54]

It may help to set Pound's deeply-held views, somewhat erratically expressed, against a philosophical context: Suzanne K. Langer's essay "The Cultural Importance of Art."[55] "The ancient ubiquitous character of art contrasts sharply with the prevalent idea that art is a luxury product of civilization, a cultural frill, a piece of social veneer. It fits better with the conviction held by most artists, that art is the epitome of human life . . . the spearhead of human development, social and individual. The vulgarization of art is the surest symptom of ethnic decline. . . . [And] language, of course, is our prime instrument of conceptual expression. . . . Words are the terms of our thinking as well as the terms in which we present our thoughts, because they present the objects of thought to the thinker himself. . . . Language gives outward experience its form, and makes it definite and clear. . . . The primary function of art is to objectify feeling so that we can contemplate and understand it. . . . Bad art is corruption of feeling. This is a large factor in the irrationalism which dictators and demagogues exploit."[56] Langer's brief but extremely pregnant analysis, even in expurgated summary, plainly fits almost perfectly with

Pound's. The cranky tone, the rambling prose, the interjections and asides, ought not to conceal from us that Pound is fighting a real battle, in a war of vast importance. When he asserts that "Great literature is simply language charged with meaning to the utmost possible degree" he is making a statement of profound truth and significance.[57] Whether we agree with his method for ranking writers, whether we find his fanciful terms for the three kinds of poetry of any utility,[58] and whether we agree with his listing (in the last half of the essay), of the writers it is necessary and advisable to read, *How to Read* is very much on the side of the angels. It may not always be easy to see its perceptivity, or to recognize its importance, but it is nevertheless a cardinal text in the struggle against all manner of tyranny.[59]

ABC of Reading is a fuller and thus inevitably a somewhat more satisfying statement of the substance of *How to Read*. As Pound notes, "The only intelligent adverse criticism of my *How to Read* was not an attack on what was in it, but on what I had not been able to put there."[60] Accordingly, *ABC of Reading* was intended to "be impersonal enough to serve as a text-book . . . that can also be read 'for pleasure as well as profit' by those no longer in school; by those who have not been to school; or by those who in their college days suffered those things which most of my own generation suffered."[61] Pound was not capable of achieving such universalist goals, though it is to his credit that he dreamed of them. Through page 92, however, *ABC of Reading* is a quirkily brilliant exposition of now familiar themes. Pages 95 through 194 are a series of annotated "exhibits," designed to give specificity to his arguments. Pages 197 through 206 are the least satisfying in the book, being a "Treatise on Metre" which is remarkable as much for what it does not say as for what it does. Only a prosodic expert can make much use (or much sense) of this last section. Though it presents nothing basically new and therefore needs little attention here, the bulk of the book is readily comprehensible, largely commonsensical, and frequently both brilliantly perceptive and great good fun. It is a book which has been undeservedly neglected.

ECONOMICS AND POLITICS

Major Clifford Douglas (1879–1952), a monetarist reformer and social tinkerer, was the author of two basic texts advocating what came to be called "social credit," *Economic Democracy* (1919) and *Credit-Power and Democracy* (1920). Social credit argues essentially that the ills of modern society, notably depressions, are really paper phenomena and can be controlled, even eliminated, by appropriate paper manipulations instituted by a knowing government. Industry created goods, but, Douglas maintained, could not create sufficient purchasing power to buy those goods. Government, accordingly, could keep the economic wheels running in good order by the simple device of dividends, issued directly to its citizens. As Eric Roll points out in his *History of Economic Thought,* the arguments of Douglas, and of those who like him thought that society could be cured of all economic disease by this or that elementary bit of manipulation, were very much a product of the after-shocks of World War One and the depression of the 1930s.[62] Neither a crank nor in the strict sense of the term an economist, Douglas later saw his doctrines prevail in two of the western provinces of Canada, Alberta and British Columbia, but without either the economic or the political success that he had predicted. After 1958 the Social Credit party lost all representation in the Canadian Parliament.

Pound too was suffering the personal and social after-shocks of World War One. His position in England had been worsening steadily; his attitude toward the British had been growing more and more negative. By June 1918, he was telling John Quinn that "the present international situation seems to me in no small measure due to the English and American habit of keeping their ostrich heads carefully down their little silk-lined sand-holes."[63] A year or so later he wrote, again to Quinn, "Have had two opulent weeks as dramatic critic on *The Outlook,* and have been fired in most caddish manner possible. Have had my work turned down by about every editor in England and America, but have never before felt a desire for vengeance."[64] In September 1920, just before leaving England for good, he told

William Carlos Williams "there is no longer any intellectual *life* in England save what centres in this eight by ten pentagonal room . . . NO literary publication extant in England." He wondered, indeed, "whether, from the medical point of view it is masochism for me even to stay here."[65] From Paris, the next spring, he told Marianne Moore "I thought I had at last got free of all Anglo-Saxon connections."[66]

Pound was ready, when in 1918 Major Douglas appeared in Alfred Orage's *New Age* office, panaceas in hand. Orage and Pound talked with him at length; Orage helped Douglas with stylistic and other writing matters.[67] It took a year or two for the new doctrines fully to take hold, but by 1920 Pound was hooked. An essay on W. H. Hudson declares:

> A bloated usury, a cowardly and snivelling politics, a disgusting financial system, the sadistic curse of Christianity work together, not only that an hundred species of wild fowl and beast shall give way before the advance of industry, i.e. that the plains be covered with uniform and verminous sheep, bleating in perfect social monotony; but in our alleged 'society' the same tendencies and the same urge that the bright plumed and fine voiced species of the genus anthropos, the favoured of the gods, the only part of humanity worth saving is attacked.[68]

It is all jumbled together—politics, economics, religion, and the "attack" on the first-class artist, "the only part of humanity worth saving." Ten years later he wrote in Eliot's magazine *The Criterion:* "C. H. Douglas is the first economist to include creative art and writing in an economic scheme, and the first to give the painter or sculptor or poet a definite reason for being interested in economics; namely, that a better economic system would release more energy for invention and design.[69]

As for Italy, and Benito Mussolini, Pound felt himself on equally sure ground. Writing to Harriet Monroe from Rapallo, November 1926, he declared that "Poetry here is decent and honourable. In America it lays one open to continuous insults on all sides, from the putridity in the White House down to the expressman who handles one's trunk . . . I personally think extremely well of Mussolini. If one compares him to American presidents (the last three) or British premiers, etc., in fact one can NOT without insulting him. If the intelligentsia don't think well of him, it is because they know nothing about 'the state', and government, and have no particularly large sense of values. Anyhow, WHAT intelligentsia?"[70] Olga Rudge had a personal interview with Mussolini the next year; he impressed her—and through her, Pound.[71] Though Pound had little use for anything Russian, political or literary, in 1928 he praised both Lenin and Mussolini as "practical men."[72] By 1935, after his only interview with Mussolini, Pound was almost overwhelmed: "Mussolini a great man," he wrote at the time, "demonstrably in his effects on event, unadvertisedly so in the swiftness of mind, in the speed with which his real emotion is shown in his face, so that only a crooked man could misinterpret his meaning and his basic intention."[73] It was a bad time for Pound, and a bad time for the world. I do not mean to excuse Pound's naive, even desperate belief, but simply to set it in the proper context. "*Damn* it all," he swore at Harriet Monroe in September 1933, "the only thing between food and the starving, between abolition of slums and decent life is a thin barrier of utterly damned stupidity re the printing of metal discs [i.e., coins] or paper strips [i.e., paper money]. 30 years ago people didn't know. It is as complex *and* as simple as Marconi's control of electricity."[74] In 1940 he told the young British poet, Ronald Duncan, "Damn it all, I am a poek [poet], partly a musician, i.e. in one corner up to a point, and an economist."[75] Later the same year he advised Katue Kitasono to consult "Ez' *Guide to Kulchur*, facilitated by Ez' system of economics, now the program of Ministers Funk and Riccardi."[76] (Walter Funk was president of the German *Reichsbank* from 1930 to 1945 and Raffaello Riccardi was an Italian economist and government official.) Just before the United States entered the war, he wrote to William Carlos Williams:

> The whole occident wants homesteads or an equivalent, plus defence of purchasing power of labour, especially agricultural. . . . The opposition that you indicate is TIME LAG, or at least you better figure out how far

there is any real opposition and how far it is Time lag
and nowt but time lag. . . . Shd welcome yr ideas as to
what I ought to think about our native land and its
rulers. Naturally you object to thinking about its govt
and prefer to consider the anthropomorphology and
composition of the humus and subsoil, but you keep
on exposin that the outcroppins result from etc or are
symptoms of.[77]

The stage was set. He had begun broadcasting over Rome
Radio in January 1941; by October he was saying "Democracy
has been LICKED in France. The frogs were chucked into war
AGAINST the Will of the people. Democracy has been licked to
a frazzle in England where it never did get a look in ANYHOW.
. . . Democracy is in her last DITCH, and if she ain't saved in
America, NO ONE is going to save her in her parliamentary
form. . . . WHAT support does the United States GET from
Anglo-Judaea?"[78] Later that month he railed against "Mr.
Churchill and that brute Rosefield [Franklin Roosevelt], and
their kike postal spies and obstructors, kikarian and/or others
[who] annoy me by cuttin' off normal mental intercourse with
my colleagues."[79] For years he had been writing letters and
sending pamphlets across the Atlantic, trying to persuade anyone, no matter of what views or position, in or out of government, that he had the answers and they could have them too,
easily, if only they would accept guidance from him. By November he was advising Americans that

"it is NOT *necessary* to have the earth ruled by senile
bleeders and swindlers. The youth of Europe has discovered that cardinal fact. . . . What I affirm is that
[Roosevelt] never showed the faintest inclination to
learn the facts and come out for a JUST solution. That is
a fairly conservative statement. He has NEVER been
neutral. . . . You Americans and the English want
government to be good without ANY effort on your
part whatever. You don't even look at what is done by
your governments. Takes an awful heave to get ANY of
your attention turned onto the vital facts of a govern-

ment policy. . . . Why should all men under forty be expected to die or be maimed in support of flagrant injustice, monopoly and a dirty attempt to strangle and starve out 30 nations?"[80]

On the day war broke out for the United States, 7 December 1941, Pound broadcast that

"Of course I don't know what GOOD I am doin', I mean what IMMEDIATE good. But something you folks on both side of the wretched ocean will have to learn, war or no war, sooner or later. . . . My politics seem to me SIMPLE. . . . What I am ready to fight AGAINST is havin' ex-European Jews making another peace worse than Versailles. . . . And the sooner all America and ALL England wake up to what the War-burgs and Roosevelt are up to, the better for the next generation and this one. . . . I do NOT want my compatriots from the ages of 20 to 40 to go git slaugh-tered to keep up the Sassoon and other British Jew rackets. . . . That is not my idea of American patriotism. . . . And NO number of Rabbis and bank touts in Wall Street and in Washington can do one damn thing for England. . . . Lord knows I don't SEE how America can have fascism without years of previous trainin'. Looks to me, even now as if the currency problem was the place to start savin' America. . . . Both sides will have to come to it.[81]

Pound then broke off his broadcasts until 29 January 1942 when, among other things, he said that "the United States had been for months ILLEGALLY at war, through what I considered to be the criminal acts of a President whose mental condition was NOT, so far as I could see, all that could or should be desired of a man in so responsible a position or office." He had "a perfectly good alibi," he explained, "if I wanted to play things safe." But what he did was spend "a month tryin' to figure things out. . . . Yaaas, I knew . . . what the war was about: gold, usury and monopoly. I had said as much when I was last in America."[82] Four days later he added: "You are in it, and Lord knows, who is a goin' to git you out. . . . A way to get yourselves OUT, might be discoverable, it might be more discoverable if you first had the faint inkling of a curiosity as to how you got yourselves IN." The war represented the "absolute collapse of the American system of government. Can we revive it? Has the country got the guts for the climb? Is there, as I am sayin' this, the faintest stirring of a desire INside the United States for any healthy new structure? . . . Thirty years war, 30 years paradise for Army contractors, may not be what you voted for. . . . And you have insulted the most highly tempered people on earth [the Japanese]. With unspeakable vulgarity you have insulted the most finely tempered people on earth. . . . You are at war for the duration of the Tenno's [The Japanese Emperor] pleasure. Nothin' in the Western World; nothin' in the whole of our Occident can help you to dodge that."[83]

Pound's American passport had been, in mid-1941, limited to use for return to the United States. His aged father had suffered a broken hip and could not easily be moved. His daughter Mary was not an American citizen, at least according to documentation readily available. His wife was of British origin, but had lost her nationality by marrying Pound. The woman he seems most to have loved, Olga Rudge, was no legal relation to him. He did consider leaving; it seems likely that the last train carrying Americans from Rome to Lisbon was, at the last minute, closed to him. Facts are elusive, except the decisive fact: Pound did not leave Italy, though his country was at war with that nation, and he went on broadcasting, in exactly the tenor I have been quoting, all through the war.

He was arrested in 1945 and confined—in a metal cage, at first—in Pisa. He was brought to the United States by air and charged formally with treason. Psychiatric testimony established his unsound mental condition; instead of being brought to trial he was ordered confined in the mental ward at St. Elizabeth's Hospital in Washington, D. C. He remained there, under gradually more relaxed circumstances, until 1958, when time and pressure from all over the world led the American government to dismiss charges and allow him, in his early seventies, to return to Italy, which he did in June of 1958.

6 A Failed But Fascinating Epic
The *Cantos*

The *Cantos*, both the most highly praised and the most roundly condemned of Pound's mature poetry, were unfinished at his death. The collected edition contains one hundred and nine completed Cantos (excluding numbers seventy-two and seventy-three, which were written in Italian) and drafts and fragments of eight more; it runs to a massive eight hundred and two pages.[1] It is in many ways a mistake to speak of them as a single poem, though Pound not only insisted from the first that they were a unity, but assured W. B. Yeats that his "immense poem . . . will, when the hundredth canto is finished, display a structure like that of a Bach Fugue." Yeats added that in Pound's more detailed accounting "There will be no plot, no chronicle of events, no logic of discourse, but two themes, the Descent into Hades from Homer, a Metamorphosis from Ovid, and mixed with these, mediaeval or modern historical characters."[2] That was in 1930. Three years earlier Pound had written to his father conceding that "the whole damn poem is rather obscure, especially in fragments," but insisting that it was "rather like, or unlike subject and response and counter subject in fugue," and had three main directions: "(1) the 'live man' going down into the world of the dead, (2) the 'repeat' in history, and (3) the 'magic moment' or moment of metamorphosis, the 'bust through' from the everyday world into the divine or permanent world of the gods."[3] Ten years still, while struggling to get the project under way, he had told James Joyce that it was "an endless poem, of no known category."[4]

Pound's essentially literary, deeply uncertain grasp of what the *Cantos* were up to, at all stages of their composition, has not stopped critics from seeing what was not there to be seen. "There is no other poetry like *The Cantos* in English," wrote Allen Tate. "And there is none quite so simple in form. The form is in fact so simple that almost no one has guessed it. . . . The secret of his form is this: conversation. *The Cantos* are talk, talk, talk; not by anyone in particular to anyone else in particular; they are just rambling talk. . . . Each Canto is a cunningly devised imitation of a casual conversation in which no one presses any subject very far. . . . The transitions between *The Cantos* are natural and easy."[5] It would be pleasant if it were all so simple, so "natural and easy"; it is not. Donald Carne-Ross, while conceding that "for long sections of *The Cantos* Pound has simply failed in his poet's job," also feels able to declare that "the subject of *The Cantos* is no less than 'all history', 'all myth', without distinction of time or place."[6] This bumbling over-enthusiasm needs to be set against T. S. Eliot's sober judgment that "In *The Cantos* there is an increasing defect of communication,"[7] or George Dekker's well-supported conclusion, in perhaps the best study of the *Cantos* yet written, that they are "a work which is neither scholarly nor poetic. . . . The poem, as a poem, is a colossal failure. . . . What is wrong finally with Pound's method is that it is based on a translator's, not a poet's, approach to the world."[8] "The Cantos," explained Maxwell Bodenheim, "represent the nervous attempt of a poet to probe and mould the residue left by the books and tales that he has absorbed, and to alter it to an independent creative effect."[9] Yvor Winters similar notes that "The details, especially in the early Cantos, are frequently very lovely, but since there is neither structure nor very much in the way of meaning, the details are details and nothing more, and what we have is the ghost of poetry, though I am willing to admit that it is often the ghost of great poetry."[10] In Glenway Westcott's words, written as early as 1925, "the Cantos are one of the most glorious of those long poems in whose construction common sense takes no part."[11] But the sharpest, clearest, and most comprehensive summary is that of Pound's biographer, Noel Stock, a man who has worked long and lovingly, as well as intimately, with Pound and his poetry:

> Early in his life Pound had dedicated himself to the writing of a masterwork and later decided that it should take the form of an 'epic' about history and civilizations. But the trouble was that the 'epic' was born of the desire to write a masterwork rather than of a particular living knowledge which demanded to be embodied in art. At no stage was he clear about what he was trying to do and further confusion was added when in the wake of Joyce and Eliot he decided that his 'epic' would have to be modern and up to date. Although he had no intellectual grasp of the work to be made he was determined nevertheless to write it. Thus persisting against the virtue of his art he lost any chance he may have had to pause and rethink the whole project and went on piecing together an endless row of fragments. Some cantos and some fragments contain high poetry and there is much that is humorous or otherwise interesting; but in so far as the work asks to be taken as a whole it verges on bluff.[12]

It is downright silly—the word is unfortunately not too strong—to speak of the *Cantos* as does a fine critic like Hugh Kenner: "Pound's structural unit in the *Cantos* is not unlike the Joycean epiphany: a highly concentrated manifestation of a moral, cultural, or political quiddity. . . . In the *Cantos* the place of a plot is taken by interlocking large-scale rhythms of recurrence. . . . The facts generalize themselves in the *Cantos*, especially the later ones, into steady patterns of athletic beauty."[13] But it is just as silly to flippantly dismiss the *Cantos* as what "may be called 'flash-card verse,' "[14] or to assert rather pompously that "One gives the Cantos respectful, purely intellectual admiration."[15] There seem to me three questions that need to be addressed: (1) What did Pound think he was doing? (2) Why? (3) How well (or how badly) did he do it? It is with these questions that this chapter is concerned.

(1) WHAT DID POUND THINK HE WAS DOING?

To some extent, as Stock explains, Pound never did know what he was doing. To the extent that he had control over his materials, however, there are reasonably clear indications both of formative influences and of developing intention. Pound wrote the first three Cantos in 1915 (they were published in 1917), but only the first two lines of Canto II, slightly expanded from the initial line of the original Canto I, survive from that early attempt.

> Hang it all, there can be but one *Sordello!*
> But say I want to, say I take your whole bag of tricks,
> Let in your quirks and tweeks, and say the thing's an
>   art-form,
> Your *Sordello,* and that the modern world
> Needs such a rag-bag to stuff all its thought in;
> Say that I dump my catch, shiny and silvery
> As fresh sardines flapping and slipping on the
>   marginal cobbles?

This is the opening of the original first Canto; the influence of Browning is plainly all over it. It is Browning's 1840 narrative, *Sordello,* which is alluded to, and Browning himself who is directly addressed.[16] Browning's poem, observes Ronald Bush, "and the [early] Cantos modeled after it, intend to be a new kind of narrative poetry—a poetry that portrays not just an action but an authentically modern dramatization of the way an action acquires significance within an individual intelligence."[17] The original Cantos, in fact, closely (and not surprisingly) resemble poems like "Near Perigord," discussed earlier. "Near Perigord" too was first published in 1915; it too tries to weave a historical canvas and simultaneously "solve" the psychological "riddle" alluded to in line four, the "broken bundle of mirrors" of the poem's final line. "Near Perigord" is inert, dull, and essentially lifeless; the "riddle" is approached almost entirely from the outside, without intimacy or passion. The three original Cantos are no better. "Let us hope you may get over your dislike of the poem," Pound wrote to Harriet Monroe, "by the time the last of it is printed." (It appeared in the June, July, and August 1917 issues of *Poetry*). After all, he adds, "you disliked 'Contemporania' and even the first of Frost himself, and you loathed and detested Eliot."[18] But there were very real problems: Eliot critiqued the poems, and Pound rewrote them, struggling to make sense of what he was doing. Considering the Browning influence, it made sense for Eliot to write in 1918 that "in appearance, [the poem] is a rag-bag of Mr. Pound's reading in various languages. . . . And yet the thing has . . . a positive coherence; *it is an objective and reticent autobiography*" (emphasis added). Eliot amplified this perception of the *Cantos* in 1919, arguing that they indicated what "the consummation of Mr. Pound's work *could* be: a final fusion of all his masks (emphasis added).[19] Neither of Eliot's observations held true of the *Cantos* as Pound subsequently evolved them, but they are deeply perceptive of the nature of the first versions.

Browning was not the only large influence. Pound's prose writings, from the period roughly contemporaneous with the early *Cantos*, exhibit an active concern with fictive techniques like dialogue, narrative, and characterization. *Indiscretions*, his incomplete prose memoir, was written shortly after World War One. It is consciously derivative from Henry James, and not only because Pound points out in his 1923 note that "there is a gap—between, that is, the place where the Great H.J. leaves off in his 'Middle Years' and the place where the younger writers try to start some sort of faithful record,"[20] but also because the mark of the Master is evident stylistically. Here is part of the second paragraph which, in its entirety, is a single sentence almost two printed pages in length:

> Whereafter two days of anaesthesia, and the speculation as to whether, in the development and attrition of one's faculties, Venice could give one again and once more either the old kick to the senses or any new perception; whether coming to the belief that human beings are more interesting than anything possible else—certainly than any possible mood of colours and footlights-like glare-up of reflection turning house fa-

cades into stage card-board; whether in one's an-
thropo- and gunaikological [gynecological?] passion
one were wise to leave London itself—with possibly a
parenthetical Paris as occasional watch-tower and alter-
nating exotic *mica salis* [morsel of salt]; and whether—
the sentence being the mirror of man's mind, and we
having long since passed the stage when 'man sees
horse' or 'farmer sows rice', can in simple ideographic
record be said to display antyhing remotely resembling
our subjectivity—and whether—to exhaust a few more
semi-colons and dashes—one would—will, now that I
am out of a too cramped room at the Albergo Bella
Venezia. . . .[21]

This is about a third of the whole, and it is enough, particularly
when Pound himself makes perfectly clear both his imitative
intent and also the basic belief, operative in his poetry as well as
in this prose, that the sentence is "the mirror of man's mind."
Pound knew Henry James's work well, and his long 1918 essay
provides, on the whole, a just and balanced estimate of that
author. But Pound's affection for James's intricately written,
frequently rather opaque and convoluted "travel book," *The
American Scene,* is as excessive as it is revealing. It is, he claims, a
"triumph of the author's long practice. A creation of America. A
book no 'serious American' will neglect."[22] More to the point,
perhaps, is W. H. Auden's observation that *The American Scene*
was not so much prose as "a prose poem,"[23] and Leon Edel's
statement that James "wrote in a vein of poetry: buildings
address him; monuments meditate; he offers us a continual
monologue, sometimes rhapsodic, often reportorial."[24] Pound's
Indiscretions is tribute, not parody, and the techniques there
practiced have clear importance for virtually all of the *Cantos.*
For while Eliot, in *The Waste Land* and elsewhere, used fragmentation and discontinuity to emphasize his belief in order, and his
"instinctive revulsion from discontinuity," Pound believed just
as deeply "that fragmentation and contradiction are a normal
part of reality at all times, present or past."[25]

Nor is *Indiscretions* the end of Pound's experiments in prose, at about this time when the *Cantos* were taking their early shape. Influenced by the "Imaginary Dialogues" of Walter Savage Landor, and by the contemporary prose experiments of Remy de Gourmont ("a man 'absorbed in . . . the struggle for the rights of personality,' " Pound wrote in 1917,)[26] he not only translated "Twelve Dialogues of Fontenelle" (1916) but wrote five prose sketches (close to but not quite the same thing as prose fiction).[27] Two are in dialogue form; "in the others," as Bush nicely says, "Pound experimented with sophisticated narrative voices to control unusual material, and to create a *stylistically interesting texture* (emphasis added).[28]

> The soul of Jodindranath Mawhwor clove to the god of this universe and he meditated the law of the Shastras. He was a man of moderate income. . . . To the Kama Sutra he had given minute attention. He was firmly convinced that one should not take one's pleasure with a woman who was a lunatic, or leprous, or too white, or too black, or who gave forth an unpleasant odor, or who lived an ascetic life, or whose husband was a man given to wrath and possessed of inordinate power. These points were to him a matter of grave religion.[29]

"I find no man a prig who takes serious thought for the language," he makes Rabelais declare in one of the dialogues, and in "Religio, or 'The Child's Guide to Knowledge'" he constructs a quasi-prophetic question-and-answer formulation, much like a religious creed:

> What is a god?
> A God is an eternal state of mind.
> What is a faun?
> A faun is an elemental creature. . . .
> When is a god manifest?
> When the states of mind take form.[30]

In a series of "Imaginary Letters" which he contributed to *The Little Review* (after Wyndham Lewis, who had begun them, was stopped from further contributions by his joining the British Army), Pound worked further at a prose "tone" which he would put to more extensive use in the *Cantos:* "People imagine that to speak suddenly, and without thinking beforehand, is to be brilliant. . . . I am a civilized man; I can put up with anything that amuses me. . . . All things pass under the nose of my microscope. I am one man without a class prejudice. It is perhaps my only distinction."[31]

Pound's work with Eliot's poetry, most famously his massive condensation of *The Waste Land* but also his proposed and not accepted suggestions for "Gerontion," also help clarify what was on Pound's mind as he struggled with the *Cantos.* I have discussed this crucial relationship elsewhere and at some length.[32] Briefly, Eliot had intended, and tried to write a much longer, more comprehensive, distinctly more socially oriented, and more narrative poem than the version which finally saw print. Pound insisted, however, on a more elliptical style and structure. "As a result of Pound's suggestions," says Bush, "the speakers of *The Waste Land* lost that degree of tangibility we usually require to 'size up' characters." He notes, too, that *"The Waste Land* would have been more satisfying had Pound allowed Eliot to expand the poem's music-hall qualities."[33] My own conclusion is that "essentially, Pound did indeed help the poem, especially considering *The Waste Land* as a narrowly literary production. But he significantly changed it as well, and as a social and a psychological document *The Waste Land* as printed is a somewhat weakened, somewhat confused affair."[34] If it were possible (for legal reasons it is not) to quote Eliot's original, pre-Poundian lines, it would be easier to establish precisely what Pound sought (successfully, on the whole) to eliminate. Bush's comments on Pound's proposed (but not accepted) revisions for "Gerontion" are helpful in this context:

> He bracketed two kinds of words for excision: (1) weak modifiers, and (2) verbs he took to be extraneous either because they were inactive ('is' or 'was') or because they were 'unnecessary' repetitions—that is, verbs that Eliot repeated from an earlier line to clarify connections. In every case, the words would not ordinarily be considered extraneous. They were connectives that, if

omitted, would have given the lines the appearance of fragmentation. Had Eliot followed Pound's suggestions, 'Gerontion' would be less comprehensible than it now is. It would also be more saliently 'Poundian', for the suggestions followed principles on which Pound had been revising his own Cantos.[35]

Bush's comments on the "structural method" of the *Cantos* essentially sums up what the preceding brief discussion has set forth: "The structural method of the *Cantos* started in an intuition and changed gradually as Pound progressed from one stage of composition to the next."[36] Pound also summed it up, after a fashion, in a December 1919 letter to his father. Each of the cantos (he had just completed V, VI, and VII) was, he wrote "more incomprehensible than the one preceding it; I don't know what's to be done about it."[37] Nor did he ever learn.

(2) WHY DID POUND DO AS HE DID IN THE CANTOS?

No one can speak for Pound. It is difficult, even given the fairly voluminous record now publicly available, to feel confident that one has successfully entered into and to any significant degree understood so complex and shifting mind as his. But a framework of explanation that is at least possible, and which is supported by the available evidence, can be suggested.

First and to some extent foremost is the matter of ambition. Pound "had grown up, like Keats a hundred years before him, with the conviction that a man cannot be a great poet unless he master the long poem. Whitman stood as an example and a challenge, and Pound had been planning an epic poem of one kind or other ever since his undergraduate days at Hamilton [College]."[38] "His first idea as a magnum opus [was], apparently, to write a trilogy on Marozia (d.945), wife of Alberic I, Prince of Rome."[39] Pound was no more fitted for such a work than William Wordsworth would have been; Wordsworth could not write the projected three parts of his philosophical epic without help, which he never received, from Samuel Taylor Coleridge. But Wordsworth could, and did, write the long poem we now call *The Prelude* (never so called by the poet himself; the poem was published only after his death, and others supplied the title). There was a willingness, arguably even an eagerness for self-examination, in Wordsworth, which was notably lacking in Ezra Pound. Eliot saw in the early versions of the *Cantos,* again, the possibility of "an objective and reticent autobiography," or, alternatively, "a final fusion of all [Pound's] masks." There are indeed autobiographical bits in the *Cantos,* some of them disguised. But there is no true autobiography, no intensive self-examination: the *Cantos* is the very farthest thing from what is sometimes called "confessional" poetry.

Pound did contemplate, and in part at least did write (and then destroy) a novel. He thought about other long narrative forms, in prose genres or in drama. But when he actually ventured into what might have been a truly fictive, truly narrative form, like "Jodindranath Mawhowor's Occupation," the first of the prose pieces later collected as *Pavannes,* he found himself unable to sustain either narrative or characterization. The piece is seven printed pages long, divided into four sections. Until almost the last paragraph the possibility of true fiction remains: the main figure and his friend, Mohon, are characterized; there is a liaison with a lady, not spelled out but carefully introduced, with subsequent reflections on relationships with women and with the world at large; there is discussion on these matters between the main character and his unnamed twelve-year-old son. And then the narrative is snuffed out, and the whole piece comes to an abrupt and unexpected end. The main character speaks his piece to his son, lies down, and falls asleep. "The next day he shaved his whole body. His life [was] not unduly ruffled." There is a paragraph of further advice to the son, and then a brief final paragraph: "His son's life was not unduly ruffled."[40] It would be too much to say that Pound was incapable of narrative. No one, least of all anyone who can handle the language as Pound could, is incapable of narrative. In fact, Pound has managed narrative in poems of his own and in many of his translations. But plainly he is disinclined toward narrative, in this prose sketch as in the *Cantos.* What interests him is not the conflict between characters or within a character, which forms what we call plot, but the conclusions to be drawn from narrative. A writer genuinely interested in fiction would ask: what happened to/in the twelve-year-old boy, after his father's preaching and in the light of his father's practice? What happened to Mawhowor himself? What happened to his friend Mohon? Pound is interested only in asserting that neither father nor son were "unduly ruffled." In a true prose narrative that would be totally conclusory, and deeply unsatisfactory. Pound does not want to write a true prose narrative, and that is the end of it. Neither the commercially viable stories he hoped and at one time planned to write, nor the collaborative detective novel he talked about, were ever written. (Or if they were written, none have survived; certainly, nothing of these projects ever appeared in print.)

The *Cantos* are not confessional, they are not narrative. What they are, as might be expected with an author so dominated by ambition and by literature, is work reflective of other literature. Pound draws on Homer in Canto I, on Browning and then again on Homer in Canto II, on the *Poema de mio Cid* in Canto III, and so on. When he runs out of literary forebears, or when he tires of them, he draws on the closest thing to the literary past, namely the historical past. Huge swatches of the *Cantos* turn into modified, half-translated, summarized, and sometimes commented-upon historical documentation. This is not, let me emphasize, the sequence that is history, nor the narrative that is history, nor the interpretation that is history, nor anything else that is history, but only the documentation of history—letters, diaries, official orders and pronouncements, and so on, all thrown together without any sort of framework.

Pound had denied himself access to his own personal past, he had denied himself the possibility of constructing a fictive narrative, he had denied himself the possibility of working within some historical narrative. Any of these possibilities could have provided him, as they had traditionally provided others, with an epic-like framework, a structure on which all sorts of shimmering detail could have been hung. He did not have religious belief; he did not believe in stories, but only in discontinuity. What was left to him, considering the driving ambition that required an outlet, but a magpie-like accumulation of detail without any framework? What was left but a pastiche of earlier epics, of bits and pieces from earlier narratives?

> And by the beach-run, Tyro,
>   Twisted arms of the sea-god,
> Lithe sinews of water, gripping her, cross-hold,
> And the blue-gray glass of the wave tents them,
> Glare azure of water, close-welter, close cover,
> Quiet sun-tawny sand-stretch,
> The gulls broad out their wings,
>   nipping between the splay feathers;
> Snipe come for their bath,
>   bend out their wing-joints,
> Spread wet wings to the sun-film,
> And by Scios,
>   to left of the Naxos passage,
> Naviform rock overgrown,
>   algae cling to its edge,
> There is a wine-red glow in the shallows,
>   a tin-flash in the sun-dazzle.

What can one say of this passage near the start of Canto II except that it is very beautiful? "Hang it all," the now revised Canto has begun, echoing the original Canto versions, "Robert Browning, / there can be but one 'Sordello.' / But Sordello, and my Sordello?" *My Sordello:* not my original poem, but my version of some earlier poem, my poem in competition with, parallel to but not detachable from that earlier poem, and other earlier poems. Pound begins the passage quoted above with Tyro, a daughter of Poseidon. But does he believe in Poseidon, or in any god of either sea or earth? What is Tyro doing there? She is there: that is what she is doing, and that is also the purpose of her being there. She is there to be described, to be moved about. Why are the gulls there? To be described. The snipe? To be described. It is all there because Pound has willed it onto the page. Cribbing from here and there, weaving bits and pieces together, he has willed that his snippets and his borrowings and his historical documents and his reflections and his musings and his preachings and everything else cohere, there on the page. The technique is more than adequate; poets with considerably less technique have written considerably more interesting poems, poems which do cohere because those lesser poets permit themselves (indeed, require of themselves) a framework of belief, or narrative, or both.

Why does a poet as demonstrably gifted, as potentially great as Pound deny himself the possibility of the great poem which meant so much to him, and on which he labored so hard for so very many years? There are never easy answers to such questions, and given Pound's enormous complexity and the long trailing disguises he spun around himself during a very long life, we are I suspect unlikely ever to truly answer the question. It is enough, certainly for now, to ask it, and to understand why it requires asking.

(3) HOW WELL (OR HOW BADLY) DOES POUND DO
WHAT HE DOES IN THE CANTOS?

Everyone—including Pound himself—has his own anthology of passages from the massive volume of *Cantos*.[41] "It has moments of great beauty," says Dekker,[42] and it makes no sense whatever to disagree. But which moments? Ernest Hemingway wrote in 1933 that "I believe I've read almost every line he ever wrote and still believe the best is in the cantos. Matter of opinion. There is . . . quite a lot of crap in the Cantos but there is some Christwonderful poetry that no one can better."[43] Which is Christwonderful and which is not?

The 802 page book is divided into eight sections, which are records of publication rather than substantive divisions. But they are indicative of some substantive shifts and are more than sufficient for our purposes. Seriatim, with their dates of collected publication, the eight sections are as follows:

1. A Draft of XXX Cantos (1930)
2. Eleven New Cantos XXXI-XLI (1934)
3. The Fifth Decad of Cantos XLII-LI (1937)
4. Cantos LII-LXXI (1940)
5. The Pisan Cantos LXXIV-LXXXIV (1948)
6. Section: Rock-Drill De Los Cantares LXXXV-XCV (1955)

7. Thrones de los Cantares XCVI-CIX (1959)
8. Drafts and Fragments of Cantos CX-CXVII (1969)

The Pisan Cantos, written for the most part while Pound was imprisoned in Pisa, under exceedingly difficult circumstances, won a Bollingen Prize and have created both enormous controversy and a small literature of criticism and commentary. They are also very much the most personal of the Cantos and have some splendid poetry. The largest quantity of splendid versifying, however, is generally considered to be in the first thirty Cantos. There are good passages in other relatively early Cantos; those which follow the Pisan Cantos are in general either prosey or thin (just as the second section, Eleven New Cantos, is almost uniformly boring), except for the surprising final fragments, some of which, though not quantitatively extensive, are as fine as anything Pound ever wrote.

Let me concentrate, accordingly, on selected passages from, first, A Draft of XXX Cantos; second, The Pisan Cantos; and finally, Drafts and Fragments of Cantos CX-CXVII. My primary purpose is to indicate the best portions of the *Cantos*, but along the way I will be obliged also to reproduce and briefly to comment upon less successful passages as well. A piecemeal approach to this most piecemeal of famous poems in English is not only sensible but, especially at first distinctly advisable, even necessary. I do not know how many people have read all 802 pages, straight through from start to finish, but it is not something to be recommended to anyone except the professional, the dedicated, or the masochistic. Whatever unity the *Cantos* have is in fact almost exclusively a technical affair, a matter of poetic voice rather than of poetic substance. In many ways we are dealing with 802 pages of poetic fragments, welded together (to the extent they are welded together at all) by a single poetic voice and not much else.

a. A DRAFT OF XXX CANTOS (1930)

> . . . Then quiet water,
>   quiet in the buff sands,
> Sea-fowl stretching wing-joints,
>   splashing in rock hollows and sand-hollows

In the wave-runs by the half-dune;
Glass-glint of wave in the tide-rips against sunlight,
    pallor of Hesperus,
Grey peak of the wave,
    wave, colour of grape's pulp,

Olive grey in the near,
    far, smoke grey of the rock-slide,
Salmon-pink wings of the fish-hawk
    cast grey shadows in water,
The tower like a one-eyed grey goose
    cranes up out of the olive grove,

And we have heard the fauns chiding Proteus
    in the smell of hay under the olive-trees,
And the frogs singing against the fauns
    in the half-light.
And . . .

The ellipses in the last line do not indicate an editorial omission: they are Pound's device for preventing resolution, for maintaining fragmentariness. Canto I ends: "So that:"; the passage above is the ending of Canto II. It is very like the passage reproduced earlier, also from Canto II: tone and substance, to the extent that there is substance, are very similar. The first of the two mythological references, "pallor of Hesperus," means no more than "evening light," Hesperus being the evening star and a conventional symbol of approaching night. Proteus, a sea god, is a shape-changer—an aptly evoked figure for a shape-changing poet writing perhaps the supreme shape-changing poem in our language.

This would be an extraordinary lyric, printed separately. Call it, say, "Twilight on the Aegean," or some such thing, and it makes about as much logical sense as any beautifully cadenced song. There is just enough suggestion of what is usually considered meaning, in the final strophe, to round off the lyric: we do not know why the fauns are "chiding Proteus," but (1) we can guess, and (2) it hardly matters, for it is something fauns might do, just as frogs might well be heard "singing against the fauns / in the half-light." What does matter is the evocation of the sea in the fading sunlight, and the peaceful rural Greek scene, and the lyric celebration of existence in such a place and under such circumstances. Not that this is a Greek poem; I know of no Greek poet, ancient or modern, who writes in this style. More to the point, neither does George Seferis, the contemporary Greek poet, who in his introduction to his own translation of three of the early Cantos declared that "It is purposeless to demand from such a poetry, where the important and the trivial have the same value, historical or chronological link. The only link which exists is the link of the poetical language."[44] And the poetical language is superb, gorgeously celebratory, magnificently marshalled. One cannot imagine 802 pages of such poetry: it would become overwhelmingly what Pound in 1920, writing to William Carlos Williams, called "Alexandrine Greek bunk, to conform to the ideas of that refined, charming, and utterly narrow she-bard 'H.D.' "[45] Or as he declared in 1917, reviewing H.D.'s newer work of that period, "She has also (under I suppose the flow-contamination of Amy [Lowell] and [John Gould] Fletcher) let loose dilutations and repetitions."[46] "Flow-contamination" is indeed le mot juste for such poetry, carried to any lengths: Pound's sense of order and structure may be deficient, but he has far too keen a sense for poetic variety to run endlessly on in the same key.

But what do the different keys of these early Cantos *mean*? Canto I, for example, employs what might be called an Anglo-Saxon (Old English) view of Homeric poetry, in contrast to the "Alexandrine" view we have just been examining. "And then went down to the ship, / Set keel to breakers, forth on the godly sea, and / We set up mast and sail on that swart ship, / Bore sheep aboard her, and our bodies also." This is in fact Pound's retranslation of a Latin translation of Homer, made (as Pound himself tells us elsewhere in the *Cantos*) by "Andrea Divus, / In . . . 1538." Most of Canto I is in this style, and from this source, though freely handled. Most of Canto II is in the style reproduced above. Canto III tells us of how "My Cid rode up to Burgos, / Up to the studded gate between two towers, / Beat with his lance butt, and the child came out, / Una niña de neuve años, / To the little gallery over the gate." The singing is truly in different keys; the poetry is—line by line—very well handled indeed. And that is all there is: poetry line by line, with no particular meaning, no larger structure. We must not under-value such dazzling poetry; so too we must not over-value it, claiming for it significances it simply does not have.

"I have seen what I have seen," Pound says (or has a character say) in Canto II. What has been seen? "Medon's face like the face of a dory [a spiny fish], / Arms shrunk into fins." Medon is a mythological name (the herald in Homer's *Odyssey*, who warns Penelope of the suitors' plot against her son, Tele-machus, is named Medon); here it is perhaps Circe, the enchant-ress who turned men into beasts, who has thus transformed the Medon of the poem, for Circe figures large in Canto I. But have not these figures out of Homer sailed on, away from Circe? This is Acoetes speaking, we are informed; he is subordinate to one Lyaeus; but critics insist that Odysseus is "the first-person speaker of the Canto," and Odysseus "is deliberately not distin-guished from Pound, and the identification is significant."[47] Significant to whom, and why? "I have seen what I have seen" seems as portentously unsignificant, in the sense of not signify-ing anything very much, as the opening lines of Canto III, "I sat on the Dogana's [the Italian customs house] steps / For the gondolas cost too much, that year." Or as portentously insignifi-cant as the prayer, early in Canto IV, "Hear me. Cadmus of Golden Prows!" Cadmus, the sower of dragon teeth and reaper of men, is a familiar figure, to be sure: we read on, to find out (hopefully) what he is doing in Pound's poem. "The silver mirrors catch the bright stones and flare, / Dawn, to our waking, drifts in the green cool light; / Dew-haze blurs." We are back in the world of Alexandrine Greek; and then it is not Cadmus but Pound's Provencal connections which return: "Vidal, / Vidal. It is old Vidal speaking, / stumbling along in the woods." Never mind how he got there: Pound put him there, Pound wanted him there, and critics are pleased to inform us that "This epic, which Pound described as 'the tale of the tribe', is also a tribal encyclopaedia, and in places resembles an archive."[48] It is surely not flippant to quote from Gilbert and Sullivan's "The Gondo-liers" the warning that "When every one is somebodee, / Then

no one's anybody!" When something is everything, when anything means all things, then nothing means anything very
much. From Vidal we pass to So-Gyoku, and Hsiang, and
Cavalcanti—and in this light the opening line of Canto V can be
seen, though it was probably not so intended, as a critical
observation: "Great bulk, huge mass, thesaurus."

There are marvellous bits embedded in this "thesaurus" of
Pound's reading, bits that literally no one in the history of
English poetry could have achieved. Pound's craft is more than
superlative, it is inimitable, as curious as that might seem for
someone who is himself constantly imitating and adapting from
other poets.

> . . . again the vision:
> Down in the viae stradae, toga'd the crowd, and arm'd,
> Rushing on populous business,
> and from parapet look down
> and North was Egypt,
> the celestial Nile, blue deep,
> cutting low barren land,
> Old men and camels
> working the water-wheels;
> Measureless seas and stars,
> Iamblichus' light,
> the souls ascending . . .

Does it matter if we know that Iamblichus was a neoplatonic
philosopher and an influence on a better-known philosopher,
Plotinus? Does it matter, more importantly, that we have been
moved by mysterious means from Ecbatan (which appears to be
in medieval Provence), to Rome, and then to Egypt? A few lines
farther on Pound offers a perfectly acceptable answer: "The fire?
always, and the vision always, / Ear dull, perhaps, with the
vision, flitting / And fading at will." One could say that "the
vision" is Pound's sense of his own huge poem; the characterization of it "flitting and fading at will" seems entirely just. All
the same, the lines quoted are beautiful: in reading the *Cantos*,
one learns to take what one can get. It may not be enough, it
may not be fully satisfying, but it is truly inimitable and quite

beautiful, and whether or not that really is enough, it is all there is. "The old voice lifts itself / weaving an endless sequence," as Pound writes in Canto VII. "And the life goes on, mooning upon bare hills; / Flame leaps from the hand, the rain is listless, / Yet drinks the thirst from our lips,/ / solid as echo, / Passion to breed a form in shimmer of rain-blur; / But Eros drowned, drowned, heavy-half dead with tears / / For dead Sicheus." Can it possibly be mere accident that so many of these marvellous little lyrics deal with mist-blurred perception, with light and heat blurring perception, with the "passion to breed a form in shimmer or rain-blur"? Pound adds (these passages are all from Canto VII), "Life to make mock of motion: / For the husks, before me, move, / / The words rattle: shells given out by shells." This was the man who had vowed at age fifteen to "know more about poetry than any man living, . . . know the dynamic content from the shell." The *Cantos* are not in the usual sense confessional, plainly enough, but in many ways they are self-reflective, they are Pound commenting on himself. "The words rattle: shells given out by shells." What has happened to the "dynamic content"? All that remains are the words, and they rattle on.

There are echoes from all over in these early *Cantos*, reminiscences of T. S. Eliot ("These fragments you have shelved [shored]," at the start of Canto VIII), delicately inserted early English lyrics ("Winter and Summer I sing of her grace," at the end of Canto VI), echoes strangely like the early prose fiction of John Dos Passos (the last lines of Canto VIII could almost be fitted in the pages of *U.S.A.*, Dos Passos's epic-like novel). By the time we reach Canto IX Pound has begun the dreary habit, at work in virtually every Canto thereafter, of translating documents—letters, reports, and so on—and openly telling us where he has taken these items from. *"Given in Rimini, this the 22nd day of December / anno domini 1454 / (in the sixth year of his age)."* "Illustrious Prince . . . believe me your faithful / PETRUS GENARIIS." "Florence, Archivio Storico, 4th Series t. iii, e / 'la Guerra dei Senesi col conte di Pitigliano." "Com. Pio II, Liv. VIII, p. 85. / Yriate, p. 288." Large chunks of these documents are given in the original Italian or the original Latin, as elsewhere we have large chunks in other languages, Greek, French, Provencal, and Chi-

nese. "Foreign words and [Chinese] ideograms both in these
two decads," Pound notes in his preface to Cantos LII-LXXI,
"and in earlier cantos enforce the text but seldom if ever add
anything not stated in the english, though not always in lines
immediately contiguous to these underlinings." If we are to take
Pound literally, as of course we have long since decided we
must never do, he is here disclaiming any large significance for
his multitudinous foreign language insertions. They "enforce,"
they underline, he says, immediately somewhat taking away
from both those modest assertions by adding that their English
counterparts are "not always in lines immediately contiguous."
For whom then are the source-identifications intended and the
foreign phrases? Pound's scholarship has been pretty freely
attacked: no historian, to my knowledge, would dream of using
Pound as any sort of guide to the correspondence of the medieval Popes, or to the Italian aristocracy of the period. In what
sense do the foreign phrases "enforce" or "underline" what
they do not add anything to, namely the English text of the
poem? If we do not understand each and every one of the
foreign language phrases, how are we to know whether they
enforce or contradict or are simply irrelevant to that English
text? If they are not contiguous to the English text, how far
distant are they? How are we to know? And why are we
expected to know? As so often in dealing with Pound, the
answer appears to be a simple "because." It is there; if we read
it, we are supposed to . . . what? Learn Chinese? Provencal?
Latin and Greek and French and German and Spanish and
Italian? *Why,* if none of this adds "anything not stated in the
english"? The questions and answers are circular; because is
because is because, to paraphrase Pound's contemporary, Ger-
trude Stein. (He called her "oedipus Gertie," in writing to E. E.
Cummings; "they did not get on," records Stock laconically.)[49]

> And they want to know what we talked about? . . .
> Both of ancient times and our own; books, arms,
> And of men of unusual genius,
> Both of ancient times and our own, in short the usual
>   subjects
> Of conversation between intelligent men.

This brief passage, from Canto XI, again illustrates Pound defining the functions and themes of his poem. But there is other material that is a good deal less ennobled. Canto XII ends with a dull bawdy tale about a sailor and a "poor whore." It is apparently meant to be funny (though why it is in the poem one cannot readily tell); it is not. In Canto XIV, similarly, we hear of "politicians. . . . Addressing crowds through their arse-holes," and "Profiteers drinking blood sweetened with sh-t"; there are also "vice-crusaders, fahrting through silk," and "the arse-belching of preachers," and a bishop, "Episcopus, waving a condom full of black beetles." Canto XV gives us the "laudatores temporis acti [praisers of times past; the phrase is from Horace] claiming that the sh-t used to be blacker and richer / and the fabians crying for the petrification of putrefaction, / for a new dung-flow cut in lozenges." Canto XV is saturated with imagery of this sort: "Infinite pus flakes, scabs of a lasting pox," at the end of one strophe, is followed by "skin-flakes, repetitions, erosions, / endless rain from the arse-hairs . . . continual bum-belch / disturbing its productions."

Lovely bits keep flashing out at us. Canto XVII opens with one: "So that the vines burst from my fingers / And the bees weighted with pollen / Move heavily in the vine-shoots." But by the time one reaches Canto XX, after pages and pages of swirling, incomprehensibly nonsequential episodes, ranting, bad jokes, and documents, it becomes time to wonder, what is it all about? "Noise of sea over shingle, / striking with: / hah hah aha thmm, thunb, ah / woh woh araha thumm, bhaaa." Some-one has been reading James Joyce's *Ulysses*—but is there more than that? By Canto XXI we have gotten to lines like "Intestate, '69, in December, leaving me 237,989 florins, / As you will find in my big green account book / In carta di capretto [bound in goat skin]; / And from '34 when I count it, to last year, / We paid out 600,000 and over, / That was for building, taxes and charity." Ten lines farther along we are transcribing letters from Thomas Jefferson: " 'Could you', wrote Mr. Jefferson, / 'Find me a gardener / Who can play the french horn?' " I have not checked to see if the quotation is accurately transcribed; it does not seem to matter. A poem with historical objectives—of some sort or other—can surely fit in the third president of the United States. But a french-horn playing gardener of the third president of the United States? We have passed well beyond considerations of mere relevancy: this is a game being made up as we play it, with only one player knowing the rules—and even he is constantly changing them as he goes along, not knowing in advance what tomorrow's rules are likely to be. It all depends on what he has been reading, and how he feels, and on other factors too tenuous to be delineated by mortal man.

There are strains of other sorts, too. "The sun's keel freighted with cloud, / And after that hour, dry darkness / Floating flame in the air, gonads in organdy, / Dry flamelet, a petal bourne in the wind." This passage from the second half of Canto XXI is forced, labored, constructed rather than either found or truly sung. Like "night of the golden tiger," some lines before it, the passage suggests a poet in trouble, struggling to find some way forward. "Confusion; / Confusion," he intones half a page along, "Yellow wing, pale in the moon shaft, / Green wing, pale in the moon shaft, / Pomegranate, pale in the moon shaft, / White horn, pale in the moon shaft"—and by this point the verse has badly degenerated, become mechanical and profoundly uninteresting. It remains mechanical and uninteresting until, suddenly, toward the end of Canto XXVII, the poetry flashes forth once more:

> Nothing I build
> And I reap
> Nothing; with the thirtieth autumn
> I sleep, I sleep not, I rot
> And I build no wall.
>   Where was the wall of Eblis
> At Ventadour, there now are the bees,
> And in that court, wild grass for their pleasure
> That they carry back to the crevice
> Where loose stone hangs upon stone.

This is spoken we are told by "tovarisch," plainly a Russian judging from the name. There is roughly a page about "the labours of tovarisch," but it does not cohere, adding nothing to the mere use of the Russian name. Why "tovarisch" has anything to do with Ventadour I do not know, because the poem does not tell me—and I am not concerned with what anyone or anything else tells me about a poem when the poem itself is inert and silent. There are many poems where silence, irrelevancy, and nonsequence are all important and meaningful. This is not one of those poems. Omission and digression and hopping and skipping about are, in the *Cantos*, only and entirely omission and digression and hopping and skipping about.

I find one more gem buried in the detritus, toward the end of Canto XXIX—the lines beginning "The tower, ivory, the clear sky / Ivory rigid in sunlight." But it does not glow as some of the truly great passages do and I will not quote it at length.

b. THE PISAN CANTOS LXXIV-LXXXIV (1948)

Basically drafted while Pound was locked up at Pisa, on a borrowed typewriter, the Pisan Cantos were not published until 1948. They do not contain fewer references and allusions than do earlier Cantos, but since Pound was without his books the references are necessarily different. They are both shorter and in some ways more poignant, for many of the references are to other writers, men with (or against whom) he had worked, and against whom he now measured himself and his lifetime's work. I count six clear references to T. S. Eliot, five to W. B. Yeats, two to William Carlos Williams, one to Ford Madox Ford, one to Whitman, even one to E. A. Robinson and one to James Whitcomb Riley. There are other references to writers and to poems. These eleven Cantos, which occupy one hundred and sixteen pages in the large *Cantos* volume, are in many ways the most personal of anything in that volume. " 'The Pisan Cantos' shows a new sense of proportion," wrote Louise Bogan at the time. "He begins to feel pity and gratitude, and he begins to smile wryly, even at himself. I cannot think of any other record by an artist or man of letters, in or out of prison, so filled with a combination of sharp day-to-day observation, erudition, and humorous insight."[50] Bogan's comments contain both basic truth, in her first two sentences, and much of that exaggerated, over-stated praise, in her final sentence, which became the hallmark of criticism of The Pisan Cantos (and which in its turn helped create an atmosphere for fiercely over-stated condemnation of both Pound and his poetry). The committee that awarded Pound the Bollingen Prize for 1948, on the basis of The Pisan Cantos, was composed of Conrad Aiken, W. H. Auden, Louise Bogan, T. S. Eliot, Paul Green, Robert Lowell, Katherine Anne Porter, Karl Shapiro, Theodore Spencer, Allen Tate, Willard Thorp, and Robert Penn Warren. Dwight Macdonald, who thought the award "the brightest political act in a dark period," also declared—and quite rightly—that this was a "distinguished" body.[51] There is no need to debate the award yet again, or to rehash the storm it created: it is time to simply examine The Pisan Cantos, which were called by the Bollingen judges "a lyrical poem, or group of lyrical poems,"[52] exactly as we have examined earlier portions of the *Cantos*.

The Pisan Cantos begin:

> The enormous tragedy of the dream in the peasant's
>   bent shoulders
> Manes! Manes was tanned and stuffed,
> Thus Ben and la Clara *a Milano*
>   by the heels at Milano
> That maggots shd / eat the dead bullock

Manes refers to the Roman word for the deified souls of the dead; Ben is Benito Mussolini who, with his mistress, was executed and then hung on display by the heels. The tone is not yet seriously different from that of earlier Cantos; there is however at least a promise of greater sequence and relevancy. "Yet say this to the Possum [T. S. Eliot]: a bang, not a whimper, / with a bang not with a whimper." This *is* a different tone, distinctly more personal if not precisely confessional. The reference is to Eliot's poem, "The Hollow Men," in which the world ends "not with a bang but a whimper." The promise of greater sequence and relevancy is fulfilled only in part. In the exceedingly long Canto LXXIV, the first of The Pisan Cantos, for example, Pound weaves in snippets of overheard conversation from the prison camp guards and inmates." 'All them g.d. m.f.

general c.s. all of 'em fascists' / 'fer a bag of Dukes' / 'the things I saye and doo' / ac ego in harum [and I am in the coop]/ so lay men in Circe's swinesty." Here the allusion to Circe is totally relevant and readily comprehensible. When in Canto LXXVI he breaks into French, it is totally relevant as well: "Le paradis n'est pas artificiel, / l'enfer non plus" [Heaven is not artificial, neither is hell]. In Canto LXXX he refers to the Battle Hymn of the Republic, interpolates a colloquial-style line from that immensely popular Civil War song, "mi-hine eyes hev," and comments immediately, "well yes they *have* / seen a good deal of it / there is a good deal to be seen / fairly tough and unblastable." In Canto LXXXIII, he breaks into totally relevant German: "Mir sagen / Die Damen / Du bist Greis, / Anacreon" [They say to me, the ladies, you're old/senile, Anacreon]. There is still disconnection, and there is a good bit of the poetic dithering of earlier Cantos. Toward the end of Canto LXXX we read: "When a dog is tall but / not so tall as all that / that dog is a Talbot / (a bit long in the pasterns?) / When a butt is ½ as tall as a whole butt / That butt is a small butt." Some twenty lines earlier Pound is led by the rhyme from one bad rhyme to another: "Oh to be in England now that Winston's out / Now that there's room for doubt / And the bank may be the nation's / And the long years of patience / And labour's vacillations / May have let the bacon come home." This is hardly prize-winning material. And there is quite enough bad mixed in with the good. The Pisan Cantos are different, but not totally different, and better, but not so much better that one can mark them out as something of a different order or genre. It is hardly surprising: "Re Ezra Pound," wrote E. E. Cummings, "poetry happens to be an art; and artists happen to be human beings. . . . Every artist's strictly illimitable country is himself."[53] Many of Pound's cherished beliefs remain on display: "and the Constitution in jeopardy / and that state of things not very new either," he declares early in Canto LXXIV, and a page later reaffirms that "with one day's reading a man may have the key in his hands." Several pages further we hear that "the yidd is a stimulant, and the goyim are cattle / in gt / proportion and go to saleable slaughter / with the maximum of docility." Some pages later he returns to his anti-Semitic ranting: "and the goyim are undoubtedly in great numbers cattle / whereas a jew will receive information / he will gather up information." In Canto LXXVI he lashes out at the English in familiar style: "and Bracken is out and the B. B. C. can lie / but at least a different bilge will come out of it / at least for a little, as is its nature / can continue, that is, to lie." He concludes this Canto with a portentous and righteous warning: "woe to them that conquer with armies / and whose only right is their power."

But the poetry is frequently brilliantly fine. Even descriptive passages, which in the earlier Cantos have a cool aloofness, for all their beauty, are here more personalized, more passionate:

> and there was a smell of mint under the tent flaps
> especially after the rain
>> and a white ox on the road toward Pisa
>>> as if facing the tower,
> dark sheep in the drill field and on wet days were clouds
> in the mountain as if under the guard roosts.

There are intense flashes of experientially founded insight: "from whom and to whom, / will never be more now than at present," "Cloud over mountain, mountain over the cloud / I surrender neither the empire nor the temples," "I don't know how humanity stands it / with a painted paradise at the end of it / without a painted paradise at the end of it," "To study with the white wings of time passing / is not that our delight / to have friends come from far countries / is not that pleasure / nor to care that we are untrumpeted?," "we who have passed over Lethe"—which is the final line of Canto LXXIV, from which all of these snippets have been taken. It would be difficult to label as wise much of the best poetry in the earlier Cantos, but much in The Pisan Cantos is without a doubt deeply and powerfully wise. "Nothing matters but the quality / of the affection— / in the end—that has carved the trace in the mind—" (Canto LXXVI), "The imprint of the intaglio [incised carving] depends / in part on what is pressed under it / the mould must hold what is poured into it." (Canto LXXIX), "remember that I have remembered, / mia pargoletta [my little one—female], / and pass on the tradition / there can be honesty of mind / without overwhelming talent" (Canto LXXX), "Learn of the green world what can be thy place / In scaled invention or true artistry, / Pull down thy vanity" (Canto LXXXI), "To have gathered from the air a live tradition or from a fine old eye the unconquered flame / This is not vanity. / Here error is all in the not done, / all in the diffidence that faltered" (Canto LXXXI), "There are no righteous wars . . . / that is, perfectly right on one side or the other / total right on either side of the battle line" (Canto LXXXII), "If deeds be not ensheaved and garnered in the heart / there is inanition" (Canto LXXXIII), "When the mind swings by a grass-blade / an ant's forefoot shall save you the clover leaf smells and tastes as its flower . . . / There is fatigue deep as the grave" (Canto LXXXIII), "Under white clouds, cielo di Pisa [Pisan clouds] / out of all this beauty something must come" (Canto LXXXIV).

Perhaps the closest thing to an epigraph, a one-line summary of the best in The Pisan Cantos, is a line early in Canto LXXVIII: "the old hand as stylist still holding its cunning." Pound is not speaking of himself here, but the application is clear. He is a wiser and warmer stylist (though never so fully humanized as other and, alas, better poets), but above all else he is a stylist. That has not changed, nor can it change. The combination of style and wisdom and *humanitas* is an immense accomplishment, if not the greatest of accomplishments—as in the lines from Canto LXXXII, "despite William [Butler Yeats]'s anecdotes, . . . Fordie [Ford Madox Ford] / never dented an idea for a phrase's sake / and had more humanitas." Pound has begun to understand certain things he had never before been able to grasp; as he admits in Canto LXXX, "Tard, très tard je t'ai connue, la Tristesse," which is perhaps best translated as "Late, very late have I known you, Sadness." And he adds, at once, "I have been hard as youth sixty years." That is, in the sixty years I have had to mature, to grow, and to understand, I have remained hard in the way that the young are, in their unripe lack of wisdom. "Now there are no more days," he perceives (Canto LXXX), "Nothing but death . . . is irreparable" (Canto LXXX). Yes, but "mind come to plenum [fullness] when nothing more will go into it" (Canto LXXVI). Still, there are elegies embedded in The Pisan Cantos, where before there were only lyrics. Let me quote the elegy that concludes Canto LXXX and be done:

> as the young lizard extends his leopard spots
>   along the grass-blade seeking the green midge
>   half an ant-size
> and the Serpentine will look just the same
> and the gulls be as neat on the pond
> and the sunken gardens unchanged
> and God knows what is left of our London
>   my London, your London
> and if her green elegance
>   remains on this side of my rain ditch
>   puss lizard will lunch on some other T-bone
>
> sunset grand couturier

c. DRAFTS AND FRAGMENTS OF CANTOS CX-CXVII (1969)

"Asked about the continuing progress of the poem [the *Cantos*] in 1962, he [Pound] replied: 'I have lots of fragments. I can't make much sense of them, and I don't suppose anyone else will'."[54] "It must be said," as Alexander puts it, "that the *Cantos* come to an end rather than that Pound finished them."[55] The first line of Canto CX, perhaps referring to Olga Rudge, speaks of "thy quiet house"; four lines farther on Pound declares that "I am all for Verkehr [sexual activity] without tyranny." There is much that is as it was before; I do not wish and I trust I do not need to refer to this unchanged verse. There is wisdom, as in The Pisan Cantos: "Nor began nor ends anything . . . the truth is in kindness" (Canto CXIV), "neither life nor death is the answer" (Canto CXV), "it coheres all right / even if my notes do not cohere" (Canto CXVI). There is in this last-cited Canto a splendid lyric much like the elegy that ends Canto LXXX, which was quoted in the last section:

> Can you enter the great acorn of light?
> But the beauty is not the madness

127

Tho' my errors and wrecks lie about me
And I am not a demigod,
I cannot make it cohere.
If love be not in the house there is nothing.
The voice of famine unheard.
How came beauty against this blackness,
Twice beauty under the elms—
   To be saved by squirrels and bluejays?

Perhaps the most poignant of all the fragments is on the very last page:

   M'amour, m'amour
      what do I love and
        where are you?
   That I lost my center
      fighting the world.
   The dreams clash
      and are shattered—
   and that I tried to make a paradiso
         terrestre.

And perhaps the most poignant single line is the very last of all: "To be men not destroyers."

7 The Spreading Net
Pound's Influence and Importance

Pound's accomplishments—as poet, as critic, even as translator—have sometimes been overstated by the zealous. But it is
virtually impossible to overstate his influence. Like him or not,
he is a titanic figure. As an agent provocateur, as a catalyst, as an
example and exhorter and an inspiration, as an editor and an
agent and a friend, as an enemy and an opponent and a symbol
and above all as a *presence,* Pound is I believe the most pervasive
single influence on poetry in the modern history of literature in
our language. That is a very large statement but hardly a tall
story, for the evidence can be viewed all over the public record.
This brief chapter is but a hasty glimpse of only a very small part
of what that record provides.

For convenience of presentation, the evidence seems best
divisible into three basic categories: (1) direct testimonials by
other writers, (2) critical formulations by writers and critics, (3)
indirect testimonial drawn from literary works. The third category is plainly the most treacherous and the least susceptible to
the sort of condensed statement possible here. Nor can it be the
evidence on which I principally rely: my first two categories will
inevitably be longer and fuller. But neither can the indirect
evidence of literature itself be safely neglected if the examination
of Pound's complex and powerful influence is to be—no matter
how briefly—summarized in any satisfactory way.

(1) DIREST TESTIMONIALS BY OTHER WRITERS

A number of such testimonials, including some by writers of
great importance, can be found in earlier pages; they will not be

repeated but merely incorporated by reference in this section. Among those that have not been introduced earlier there are potent acknowledgments both from those ill disposed as well as from those well disposed to Ezra Pound. Robert Frost, briefly friendly, was thereafter suspicious at best and frequently hostile (though to his credit he helped a great deal in the effort to have Pound freed from St. Elizabeth's Hospital after World War Two). At the time of their personal rupture—which had begun to take such physical form as Pound actually throwing Frost over his head, in what purported to be a friendly demonstration of jujitsu[1]—Frost wrote a free-verse letter, half parody and half protest, intending to mail it to Pound. F. S. Flint convinced him not to send it, but Frost kept the letter, which he ultimately gave to the Dartmouth College Library with instructions not to reveal it until after his death. "I was willing to take anything you said from you / If I might be permitted to hug the illusion / That you like my poetry / And liked it for the right reason. . . . / All I asked was that you should hold to one thing / That you considered me a poet."[2] There is more, including the admission that Frost feared the other poet. Two decades later Frost wrote his daughter, Lesley, advising her on what to say—and what not to say—in a talk on poetry she was to give in Cambridge, Massachusetts. "But whatever you do," he cautioned, "do Pound justice as the great original." Five years later he notes to the same correspondent that while the great majority of the human race could do nothing with editors, Pound was an exception: "Only the bullying power of an Ezra Pound ever thrust poems down a publishers throat."[3] Allen Tate, similarly, recorded in 1949 that "Insofar as [Pound] has noticed my writings at all, in conversation and correspondence . . . he has noticed them with contempt." All the same, Tate went on, "As a result of observing Pound's use of language in the past thirty years I had become convinced that he had done more than any other man to regenerate the language, if not the imaginative forms, of English verse." Nor was this a newly formulated position. In 1931 he had written of the *Cantos* that "this is the poetry which, in early and incomplete editions, has had more influence on us than any other of our time; it has had an immense 'underground' reputation. And deservedly."[4]

It is against such almost reluctant but compelling praise that we must set the most powerfully pitched, and most authoritative, praise of all, that by T. S. Eliot:

> A man who devises new rhythms is a man who extends and refines our sensibility; and that is not merely a matter of 'technique.' I have, in recent years [this was written in 1928], cursed Mr Pound often enough; for I am never sure that I can call my verse my own; just when I am most pleased with myself, I find that I have caught up some echo from a verse of Pound's. . . . He has enabled a few other persons, including myself, to improve their verse sense; so that he has improved poetry through other man as well as by himself. I cannot think of anyone writing verse, of our generation and the next, whose verse (if any good) has not been improved by the study of Pound's. His poetry is an inexhaustible reference book of verse form. There is, in fact, no one else to study."[5]

The power to catch and hold the memories, and in particular the auditory memories of other poets, is indeed one of Pound's enduring attributes. "The reason . . . why I turn to your stuff," Archibald MacLeish confessed directly to Pound in 1926, "is that I do there *hear*. Speech beautifully. Lang-uage. Put it better. And if I steal, as I swear I never till this time did, a rhythm from your lines it is half willfully as knowing wherein excellence, and half unwilled as after long talk the voice fall." MacLeish's next letter to Pound begins, "Ezrascibilissimus the Precise." And in the following letter, after acknowledging Pound's detailed and extremely helpful criticisms, MacLeish notes that "the fundamental point of your criticism in my case is that I have not found my own speech. . . . [But] everywhere I arrived I arrived at your pace and everything I found out for myself I immediately found out more or less as you would have seen it. Nothing seemed fresh or real to me, nothing seemed my own, which didn't come that way. All of which is shameful. I admit it here to myself for the first time. . . . Your suggestion for a cure is, I know, sound. The trouble is that its you I've got to get over."[6] Hart Crane, seven years younger than MacLeish (who was seven years younger than Pound) records the same sort of thing. Writing to Gorham Munson in 1921 he talks of a new picture, "a young girl's head that brings Pound's sonnet lines persistently into my head,—'No, go from me. I have left her lately. I will not spoil my shield with lesser brightness.—' You know how it goes."[7] Much younger poets have felt exactly the same outreach of power: "Read Pound aloud," Sylvia Plath wrote in her diary in 1959, "and was rapt. A religious power given by memorizing."[8] "The only bright moment I remember," Horace Gregory observes in his autobiography, "was carrying back to President Street a copy of Ezra Pound's *Personae*. It had taken me a long time to scrape up the money to buy it."[9] Writing home to his mother in 1919 a very young Hart Crane asked: "Will you do something for me? I wish you would send me via parcel post these volumes which you will find up in my room on front shelves:—'Lustra, poems' by Ezra Pound, 'Complete Poetical Works of Swinburne', and the 'Portrait of the Artist as a Young Man', by James Joyce."[10]

These tributes need to be set against the niggling and rather vacuous treatment of K. L. Goodwin in a study entitled *The Influence of Ezra Pound*. To show how Pound was regarded in England in the 1920s, Goodwin cites a comment by the intensely hostile Robert Graves to the effect that Pound's reputation was "sinking." And to show the same thing for the United States, "a young American poet, Maurice Lesemann," is quoted as having written in 1927 that "so far as I can tell they do not think of [Pound]. I find no curiosity about him among young people who read or write poetry. Only here and there one runs across some vague knowledge of him. But he is spoken of without enthusiasm."[11] I have never heard of Mr. Lesemann, but I am unavoidably reminded of a report published in 1928 on the state of poetry in Connecticut—a volume-length report which did not once mention the name of Wallace Stevens. Goodwin does his best, too, to show that Yeats's acknowledgment of help received means little or nothing. "If the effects of [Pound's] 'going over' are virtually indiscernible in the revised version of the poems concerned, why does Yeats mention it? The answer is probably that one is taking too naive a view of influence to expect Pound to have an effect on the actual construction or content of any particular poem." He adds, in another context: "These are minor matters, but they have the importance of showing the extent of Pound's influence on Yeats in stylistic matters."[12] On the contrary, Yeats is not known to have been a notably generous man in literary matters and his acknowledgment is cast in the most specific terms. "To talk over a poem with him"—these comments have been quoted earlier but need reiteration here—"is like getting you to put a sentence into dialect. All becomes clear and natural." Goodwin's preconceptions tangle him in a web of suppositions and contradictions: why did Yeats later visit Pound in Italy, and submit a new manuscript to him? Goodwin says that "Yeats's visit suggests that he did expect to get some help from Pound," but on the next page insists that "It is quite obvious that Yeats had no intention of taking his advice." Further, "It can be said with some confidence that Pound had almost no influence on Yeats during the winters spent in Rapallo."[13] Why then did Yeats keep travelling there, and keep showing Pound manuscripts? "Yeats was worried in 1933 and 1934 because it was a couple of years since he had written verse. [He was then approaching seventy.] He decided to force himself to write, and then to seek advice about the results."[14] But one can prove almost anything utilizing such techniques of analysis. Even in dealing with T. S. Eliot's *The Waste Land*, Goodwin niggles away: "In almost every case, Eliot offered an alternative reading, which Pound accepted." And, "Eliot was so grateful for Pound's help in gaining publication that he over-estimated the extent of Pound's influence."[15]

A counter comment from one who had personally experienced that influence, a poet slightly younger than either Eliot or Pound, may be helpful in clearing the air:

> Be it said of this peppy gentleman that, insofar as he is responsible for possibly one-half of the most alive poetry and probably all of the least intense prose committed, during the last few years, in the American and English language, he merits something beyond the incoherent abuse and inchoate adoration which have become his daily breakfast food . . . that insofar as he is

one of history's greatest advertisers he is an extraordinarily useful bore.[16]

When he first met Pound the next year, E. E. Cummings added in a letter to his parents: "Altogether, for me, a gymnastic personality. Or in other words somebody, and intricate." "I have for some years been an admirer of Pound's poetry," he emphasized two years later, and by 1934 Cummings felt strongly enough to reply to a Washington bureaucrat seeking advice on how the federal government might help writers, "I happen to feel that there exists one way of 'helping' creators; which is, not hindering them: and that there exists one way of not hindering them; which is, abolishing 'censorship' / / after proudly issuing which Emancipation Proclamation, the President of the United States may humbly request Ezra Pound to take charge of America's 'arts'."[17] Or as Louise Bogan, a poet three years younger than Cummings, put it in 1940, "One must realize that [Pound] is in many ways a great figure. He did an extraordinary job thirty years ago of bringing life to English verse, and his influence has not yet petered out."[18] So too John Berryman, of the next generation of poets, who termed Pound's work "one of the dominant, seminal poetries of the age."[19] And Allen Ginsberg, of the generation following Berryman's:

> the greatest poet of the age! Greatest poet of the age. . . . The one poet who heard speech as spoken from the actual body and began to measure it to lines that could be chanted rhythmically without violating human common sense, without going into hysterical fantasy or robotic metronomic repeat, stale-emotioned echo of an earlier culture's forms, the first poet to open up fresh new forms in America after Walt Whitman—certainly the greatest poet since Walt Whitman.[20]

Is it possible to deny Pound's immense influence after such statements from the poets of several generations who have themselves felt that influence? Pound "brought us immediately to the context of how to write," affirms the poet Robert Creeley. "It was impossible to avoid the insistence he put on *precisely*

134

how the line *goes*, how the word *is*, in its context, what *has been* done, in the practice of verse—and what *now* seems possible to do."[21] "He gives the practicing poet," declares Denise Levertov, "not a rigid syllabus, despite his several overlapping lists of essential reading, but examples of various virtues and possibilities against which we may learn to test our own predilections (in reading), our own powers (in writing). . . . Both in his prose and in his poetry—by precept and example—Pound teaches me not to accept received ideas without question, but to derive my own from concrete detail observed and felt, from my own individual experience. . . . He stirs me into a sharper realization of my own sensibility. I learn to desire not *to know what he knows* but to *know what I know*; to emulate, not to imitate."[22] This seems to me as powerful an acknowledgment of influence as any poet could wish. Wallace Stevens turns things on their head, but ends I think by saying exactly the same thing: "[I] have purposely held off from reading highly mannered people like . . . Pound," he told Richard Eberhart in 1954, "so that I should not absorb anything, even unconsciously."[23] Theodore Roethke, too, made "a point of saying that he has never worked much with Eliot, Pound, Moore, or Stevens."[24] Poets who walk so carefully around an eminence do so in full knowledge of just how tall and impressive it is: Mr. Goodwin might have recalled that Marianne Moore once said of Pound that he was "more the artist than anyone I've ever met."[25] Or that John Berryman, when discouraged by his first book's reception, kept repeating to himself Pound's phrase, "It is extremely important that great poetry be written but it is a matter of indifference who writes it." Berryman half seriously planned to have these words printed in large letters and hung over his desk.[26] Indeed, can one reach more directly and immediately into other poets' lives than that?

(2) CRITICAL FORMULATIONS BY WRITERS AND CRITICS

"Pound's achievement in and for poetry was threefold: as a poet, and as a critic, and also as a befriender of genius through personal contact. The least that can be claimed of his poetry is that for over fifty years he was one of the three or four best poets writing in English. During a crucial decade in the history of modern literature, approximately 1912 to 1922, Pound was the most influential and in some ways the best critic of poetry in England or America. He had an almost unerring eye for quality. . . . He developed principles of style which he conveyed to other poets in instructions that were intensely practical and specific. These had a large impact on style and form and still throw a spell over young poets. . . . Without his harassed ingenuity, some of the brilliant literature of the early twentieth century could not have been written."[27]

This calm but impressive formulation comes from the first volume of David Perkins's *A History of Modern Poetry*, a work which, when complete, will be the standard critical and historical study on the period. Professor Perkins has read and understood everything; he plays no favorites, he has no axe to grind—unlike Sir Edmund Gosse (1849-1928) who was enormously devoted to "the literary stock market . . . , carefully advancing some reputations and nibbling away at others. Among younger writers he was chiefly interested in the poets. He approved of Edith Sitwell and Siegfried Sassoon, but drew the line at 'that preposterous American filibuster and Provencal charlatan', Ezra Pound."[28] Nor are Pound's determined detractors in any way limited to the English or to members of an older generation: Harry Levin, the American comparatist, refers to Pound with consistent contempt as a "polyglot fugleman" for American avant-garde expatriots, and as "a self-avowed anti-Whitman, whose fastidious stylizations ended in an unpatriotic confusion of tongues and loyalties."[29] Graham Hough, a younger British critic, snipes in similarly dogged fashion: "Pound's idea of the study of literature as the study of technical invention," he observes, has "shrewdness and wit" but much more "tinny assertiveness." Pound's poetry strikes him as somewhat better, but "the rhythms of *Propertius* certainly incline to tenuity," and Pound's statement about his metrical objectives in that cycle of half-translations "lets in a fitful gleam rather than a flood of light." His "poetry suffers, even on the level on which it functions so persuasively and brilliantly, from the lack of any other level."[30] Hough attacks Pound from the right, Philip Rahv from the left, arguing that "his limitations are overwhelming . . . [and] should suffice to shatter the Pound cult, were it not for the fact that the cultists and their leading hierophant, Hugh Kenner, in their highly suspect, devious ideological bias and vain exegetical ardor had not already proven themselves immune to critical argument."[31] Leslie Fiedler, attacking from all directions at once, says that "in his name aspiring young poets have been taught fanatically to avoid rhyme, as well as traditional or, indeed, any clearly identifiable, easily scannable meters." The revolt against the iamb is, to Fiedler, a "threadbare Poundian injunction," and "Make it new!" was "even as he said it . . . [a] revolutionary injunction . . . in the process of becoming an iron restriction."[32] It is hard for Pound to emerge unscathed when a man a scant generation his junior remembers and describes him in these mutually conflicting terms:

> Pound's critical exposition was often fuzzy, though his intuitive taste was keen; my friends and I admired his early volumes of lyrics, *Personae* and *Lustra*, for their terse, stripped-down, neo-classical language, which made Ezra Pound unique among poets writing in English—our great "decadent" as we called him then. . . . [But] Pound even then seemed to be living in a world of his own illusions, formed by the books he was reading in Provencal, Italian, or Chinese . . . divorced from the realities of this world. . . . His idea of the poet's function was still that of the 1890 decadents. He was striking attitudes, making words play with each other . . . still weeping into his wine glass and railing at his fatherland.[33]

But Perkins is not the only critic to attempt a more balanced approach to this often bafflingly multiplex man. R. P. Blackmur asked in 1946 "What is Pound's class [i.e., his place in literature], and how can it be described without any contemptuousness in the description and without giving the effect of anything contemptible in the class; for it is an admirable class and ought to be spoken of with admiration." Blackmur then answers his own query: "Essentially it is the class of those who have a care for the purity of the tongue as it is spoken and as it sounds and as it changes in speech and sound, and who know that that purity can only exist in the movement of continuous alternation between the 'faun's flesh and the saint's vision', and who know, so, that the movement, not the alternatives themselves, is the movement of music. . . . Poets like Pound are the executive artists for their generation . . . [and] poets of the class in which Pound shines are of an absolute preliminary necessity for the continuing life of poetry."[34] This is not an exalted view of Pound's role and importance, but it is judicious and tries hard to be fair. A much younger critic, Richard Kostelanetz, distinctly an advocate of the "new," similarly offers a measured appraisal, though from very totally different perspectives:

> For all of Pound's influence upon the profession of poetry, his work has scarcely affected the general public, although certain attitudes and linguistic devices have passed through lesser poets to the larger audience. (Some of this circuitous intellectual influence has been lamentable, because neither Pound's thought nor his poetry are especially wise.) . . . Poetry magazines are still founded in the Poundian mold. . . . It is appropriate perhaps that the most sophisticated new anthology of post-1910 U.S. poetry . . . should be dedicated to Pound. . . . Rare is the contemporary poet who can write more than twenty pages without appropriating Poundian compositional devices. [But] *The Cantos* can also be cited to rationalize obscurity, in addition to all kinds of creative self-indulgence, sheer stupidity, and intellectual formlessness, so that more bad poetry in America today is indebted to Pound than anyone else.[35]

One does not need to agree with Kostelanetz in every detail to appreciate the care and intelligence of his commentary. That superb critic, Randall Jarrell, is equally balanced and fair to the *Cantos*:

> Gertrude Stein was most unjust to Pound when she called that ecumenical alluder a village explainer: he can hardly *tell* you anything (unless you know it already), much less explain it. He makes notes on the margin of the universe. . . . Some of the poetry is clearly beautiful, some of the history live: Pound can pick out, make up, a sentence or action that resurrects a man or a time. Many of Pound's recollections are as engaging as he is; his warmth, delight, disinterestedness, honest indignation help to make up for his extraordinary misuse of extraordinary powers. . . . His obsessions, at their worst, are a moral and intellectual disaster and make us ashamed for him. . . . What is worst in Pound and what is worst in the age have conspired to ruin *The Cantos* and have not succeeded.[36]

Sturdy Edmund Wilson, though less gifted in dealing with poetry than with prose, realized in 1932, after missing the opportunity, that "I should have been glad to pay my respects to Pound, who meant a great deal to the writers of my generation in America. In spite of his expatriation, which I deplored, and the rather meager and bookish fare with which his poetry always seemed to me to be nourished, he was one of the few American writers of his time who represented genuinely high standards and never let us down."[37] Pound as a promoter and literary entrepreneur is extensively summarized by Frederick J. Hoffmann: "In his critical writings, his letters, his maneuverings with magazines, he was concerned about every aspect of the writer's world: the price of books, the dispositions of publishers, the economic support of artists, censorship; above all, the formulation and defense of an aesthetic, which he wanted to make as practical and as clearly incisive as possible. . . . Pound was motivated by the purest of disinterested conviction: that . . . nothing was more important than this, for the artist was morally and culturally the arbiter and the 'savior' of a race."[38] Horace

Gregory adds that "he was less tactful than irresistible—and as a critic and teacher, less pedantic than highhanded and spirited. . . . Like a knight-errant he pricked and exploded inflated literary reputations and fought the standards of merely 'popular taste,' as well as the accepted values of middle-class, middle-brow culture."[39]

Two convinced Poundians, the classicist and comparatist W. R. Johnson and that most Poundian of all Poundians, Hugh Kenner, need to be invoked to conclude this section. Johnson says that "Pound's passion for *communitas* ["the vision of community and identity," as he defines it in writing of Walt Whitman] was extraordinary both for its intensity and for its delicacy, and his reverence for fertility and renewal, beautifully rendered page after page, is among the most precious things in modern poetry."[40] Johnson is clearly sensitive to values, and to accomplishments, in Pound that few other critics have either perceived or so surehandedly formulated. Kenner, who has written voluminously and not always evenhandedly about Pound, has in one of his less-known volumes given us the following tempered evaluation:

> Ezra Pound has stood accused of fake erudition; of wanton misunderstanding of such matters as Chinese poetics; of imposing values by the sheerest assertion. . . . Pound knew less than he wanted to, and often, through impetuosity, less than he thought he did; Pound imposed by the sheer authority of his manner; Pound had better not be one's mentor, beyond appeal, on questions of scholarly fact. But he believed, with purity of heart, in what he was doing . . . [and] purity of intention lies at the center of American achievement; it will cover, as in perhaps no other national literature, a multitude of lapses.[41]

(3) INDIRECT TESTIMONIAL DRAWN FROM LITERARY WORKS

In much of the poetry influenced by Pound one does not have to look long or hard; the influence leaps out of the page. Charles Olson's never-completed "epic," *The Maximus Poems*, is

so plainly modelled on the *Cantos* that mere citation establishes
what no commentary is required to assert:

> Off-shore, by islands hidden in the blood
> jewels & miracles, I, Maximus
> a metal hot from boiling water, tell you
> what is a lance, who obeys the figures of
> the present dance

the thing you're after
may lie around the bend
of the nest (second, time slain, the bird! the bird!

And there! (strong) thrust, the mast! flight
> (of the bird
> o kylix, o
> Antony of Padua
> sweep low, o bless

the roofs, the old ones, the gentle steep ones
on whose ridge-poles the gulls sit, from which they
    depart,

> And the flake-racks

of my city!

Olson is a considerable poet in his own right; neither his
versification nor the form and shape of his poem can be imag-
ined without the prior example of Pound.

There are however subtler if equally significant influences,
as for example in the work of a poet who should be far better
known than he is, George Oppen:

> The knowledge not of sorrow, you were
>   saying, but of boredom
> Is—aside from reading speaking
>   smoking—
> Of what, Maude Blessingbourne it was,
>   wished to know when, having risen,
> "approached the window as if to see
>   what really was going on";
> And saw rain falling, in the distance
>   more slowly,

> The road clear from her past the window-
> glass——
> Of the world, weather-swept, with which
> one shares the century.

Or in the work of a poet less known even than Oppen, though he won the American Book Award for 1982 with *Life Supports*, William Bronk (the poem is entitled "To Praise the Music"):

> Evening. The trees in late winter bare
> against the sky. Still light, the sky.
> Trees dark against it. A few leaves
> on the trees. Tension in their rigid branches as if
> —oh, it is all as if, but as if, yes,
> as if they sang songs, as if they praised.
> Oh, I envy them. I know the songs.
>
> As if I know some other things besides.
> As if; but I don't know, not more
> than to say the trees know. The trees don't know
> and neither do I. What is it keeps me from praise?
> I praise. If only to say their songs,
> say yes to them, to praise the songs they sing.
> Envied music. I sing to praise their song.

Like Oppen, Bronk does not sing in Pound's voice, nor with Pound's forms or versification; the influence is considerably less blatant than it is in Olson. And the influence has been well and fully digested in both Oppen and Bronk; what Pound wanted, indeed, was not disciples but colleagues, poets who shared his vision rather than his precise methods and exact concerns. What he wanted, as I think these examples help to show, is often exactly what he got. For as Mario Praz informs us, speaking of Pound's translations but in words applicable to his poetry and criticism as well, "he had the power of bringing to life the Provencal and early Italian poets. . . . Pound could give to his Dante that flavour of experience for which one would vainly seek in the pages of orthodox scholars."[42] Or orthodox transla-tors. Or orthodox poets. "Ezra was nice and kind and friendly and a beautiful poet and critic."[43] Of which of us can as much be said?

Notes

CHAPTER 1

1. *Lawrence in Love: Letters from D. H. Lawrence to Louie Burrows*, ed. James T. Boulton (Nottingham, England: University of Nottingham Press, 1968), 46.

2. Ezra Pound, *Gaudier-Brzeska: A Memoir* (London: John Lane, 1916; reprint, New York: New Directions, 1970), 98.

3. H.D., *End to Torment: A Memoir of Ezra Pound*, ed. Norman Holmes Pearson and Michael King (New York: New Directions, 1979), 22–23.

4. *The Letters of Ezra Pound, 1907-1941*, ed. D. D. Paige (New York: Harcourt Brace, 1950), xix.

5. Ernest Hemingway, not one ever to praise lightly, began a letter to Pound, dated 10 February 1924, "Dear Prometheus," Ernest Hemingway, *Selected Letters, 1917-1961*, ed. Carlos Baker (New York: Scribner's, 1981), 110.

6. *Pound/Ford, The Story of a Literary Friendship: The Correspondence between Ezra Pound and Ford Madox Ford and Their Writings About Each Other*, ed. Brita Lindberg-Seyersted (New York: New Directions, 1982), 87.

7. Carl Sandburg, "The Work of Ezra Pound," *Poetry* 7 (February 1916): 249–57, quoted from *Ezra Pound: The Critical Heritage*, ed. Eric Homberger (London and Boston: Routledge and Kegan Paul, 1972), 112.

8. *Literary Essays of Ezra Pound*, ed. T. S. Eliot (London: Faber and Faber, 1954), xi.

9. F. R. Leavis, "Pound in his Letters," *Scrutiny* 18 (1951), quoted from *Ezra Pound: A Critical Anthology*, ed. J. P. Sullivan (Harmondsworth, England: Penguin Books, 1970), 217.

10. Ezra Pound, *ABC of Reading* (New Haven, Conn.: Yale University Press, 1934; reprint, New York: New Directions, 1956), 32.

11. Pound, *Gaudier-Brzeska*, 113–14.

12. Ezra Pound, *Selected Prose, 1909-1965*, ed. William Cookson (New York: New Directions, 1973), unpaginated foreword.

13. Pound, *Letters*, 22.

14. Letter to Margaret Anderson of *The Little Review,* quoted from Alan Levy, *Ezra Pound: The Voice of Silence* (Sag Harbor, N.Y.: The Permanent Press, 1983), 46.

15. Robert Sencourt, *T. S. Eliot: A Memoir* (London: Granstone Press, 1971), 61.

16. Noel Stock, *The Life of Ezra Pound* (New York: Pantheon, 1970; reprint, San Francisco: North Point Press, 1982), 95.

17. H.D., *End to Torment,* 3.

18. Homberger, *Ezra Pound,* 35–36.

19. Stanley Weintraub, *The London Yankees: Portraits of American Writers and Artists in England, 1894-1914* (New York: Harcourt Brace Jovanovich, 1979), 266.

20. Ibid., 356.

21. T. S. Eliot, "Ezra Pound," *Poetry* 68 (September 1946): 326–38, quoted from *Ezra Pound: A Collection of Critical Essays,* ed. Walter Sutton (Englewood Cliffs, N.J.: Prentice-Hall, 1963), 22.

22. Weintraub, *London Yankees,* 364.

23. Hemingway, *Letters,* 113.

24. Quoted from Sven Birkerts, "Living in the Breach," *New York Review of Books,* 17 February 1983, 13.

25. G. S. Fraser, "Pound: Masks, Myth, Man," in *An Examination of Ezra Pound: A Collection of Essays to be presented to Ezra Pound on his 65th birthday,* ed. Peter Russell (London: Peter Nevill, 1950), 184.

26. H.D., *End to Torment,* 20.

27. Ezra Pound, *Pavannes and Divagations* (New York: New Directions, 1958), 14. The essay "Indiscretions" was first published in 1923.

28. Stock, *Life of Ezra Pound,* 3.

29. Pound, *Pavannes and Divagations,* 8.

30. Ibid., 15.

31. Stock, *Life of Ezra Pound,* 3.

32. Pound, *Letters,* 19–20.

33. Ibid., 29.

34. Pound, *Pavannes and Divagations,* 8.

35. Ibid., 13.

36. Ibid., 30–31.

37. Ezra Pound, "How I Began" (1913), quoted from C. David Heymann, *Ezra Pound: The Last Rower* (New York: Viking, 1976), 10.

38. There is some uncertainty about just when this sequence of events actually took place. See Stock, *Life of Ezra Pound,* 40-44.

39. Quoted from Heymann, *Ezra Pound,* 15.

40. Ibid.

41. Quoted from Stock, *Life of Ezra Pound,* 59.

42. Ibid.

43. Quoted from Homberger, *Ezra Pound,* 44.

44. Ibid., 47. Pound had by then met Flint, one of the cofounders of the so-called Imagist movement.

45. Ibid., 48.

46. Quoted from Stock, *Life of Ezra Pound*, 78.

47. Lindberg-Seyersted, *Pound/Ford*, 8. In December 1912 Pound declared that "I would rather talk poetry with Ford Madox [Ford] than with any man in London." Quoted from Stock, *Life of Ezra Pound*, 127.

48. Stock, *Life of Ezra Pound*, 109.

49. Quoted from Homberger, *Ezra Pound*, 98.

50. Stock, *Life of Ezra Pound*, 123.

51. Ezra Pound, *Patria Mia* (London: Ralph Fletcher Seymour, 1913; reprinted in *Selected Prose*, 1973), 102, 104, 107. "I have put belief in Utopias afar from me," Pound declared at the start of part two of this work (p. 125): he could not have been more profoundly in error.

52. Stock, *Life of Ezra Pound*, 124.

53. Ibid., 130.

54. Quoted from Homberger, *Ezra Pound*, 69.

55. Ibid., 81.

56. Ibid., 82.

57. Ibid., 84

58. Ibid., 140.

59. Ibid., 467.

60. J. P. Sullivan, *Ezra Pound and Sextus Propertius* (Austin: University of Texas Press, 1964), 24.

61. Donald Monk, "How to Misread: Pound's Use of Translation," in *Ezra Pound: The London Years: 1908-1920*, ed. Philip Grover (New York: AMS Press, 1978), 74.

62. Stock, *Life of Ezra Pound*, 177.

63. Ibid., 207–8.

64. Quoted from Homberger, *Ezra Pound*, 130.

65. Ibid., 200. May Sinclair similarly wrote in May 1920 that "with one exception, every serious and self-respecting magazine is closed to this most serious and self-respecting artist," ibid., 180.

66. Maxwell Bodenheim, "The Isolation of Carved Metal," *The Dial* 52 (January 1922), 87–91, quoted from Homberger, *Ezra Pound*, 203.

67. Quoted from ibid., 145.

68. Ibid., 148.

69. Ibid., 152. The essay was published in *Poetry* (January 1920).

70. Hemingway, *Letters*, 331.

71. Randall Jarrell, "Five Poets," *Yale Review* 46 (September 1956): 103–6, quoted from Homberger, *Ezra Pound*, 441.

72. *"Ezra Pound Speaking": Radio Speeches of World War II*, ed. Leonard W. Doob (Westport, Conn.: Greenwood Press, 1978). This fat and infinitely depressing volume runs to over four hundred pages.

73. Pound, *Selected Prose*, unpaginated foreword (dated 4 July 1972).

74. 1963 interview with Grazia Levi, quoted from Heymann, *Ezra Pound*, 276.

75. Ibid., 297.
76. Ibid., 271.

CHAPTER 2

1. They had been engaged. Her memoir of him, *End to Torment*, indicates that fifty years later she remained more than half in love. She there records that in 1911 Pound was capable of acting toward her much like either an older brother or a father (p. 8). Some years later, when she had just given birth to her second child, Pound visited the nursing home and announced to her that "My only criticism is that this is not my child" (p. 30). "Hilda's Book" is printed as an appendix to *End of Torment* (pp. 67–84).

2. Edmund Clarence Stedman, *An American Anthology, 1787–1900* . . . (Boston: Houghton Mifflin, 1900). Note that this is *not* the Margaret Fuller better known to history as friend and colleague of Ralph Waldo Emerson.

In his sober introductory essay the editor, who was even more the contemporary tsar of American poetry than was William Dean Howells the contemporary tsar of American prose, demonstrates high seriousness but a grimly narrow perspective. Though he consciously strives to praise, and to value, what he calls "elevation," it is clear that "taste [and] charm" are what he most cherishes in America's "bards." As Pound put it, in *Patria Mia* (1913), "It is well known that in the year of grace 1870 Jehovah appeared to Messrs Harper and Co. and to the editors of 'The Century', 'The Atlantic', and certain others, and spake thus: 'The style of 1870 is the final and divine revelation. Keep things always just as they are now'. And they, being earnest, God-fearing men, did abide by the words of the Almighty, and great credit and honour accrued unto them," Pound, *Selected Prose*, 112.

3. Stedman's encyclopedic net had hauled in five early poems by E. A. Robinson, nine by Stephen Crane, and six by Paul Lawrence Dunbar. In his double-columned, small-print pages, however, such small doses of poetic reality are swamped in wave after wave of Victorian slush. Edith Matilda Thomas, e.g., has seventeen poems in the anthology; George Edward Woodberry has sixteen; Richard Watson Gilder has eighteen; Thomas Bailey Aldrich has twenty-seven; and Stedman even prints fifteen of his own poems, covering seven full double-columned pages.

4. What Stedman-type sonnet could have featured a trimeter line like "As little winds that dream"?

5. The cadence also shows an interesting similarity to mature work by Robert Frost.

6. I omit here *Provenca* (1910), poems called from his first three volumes.

7. I am not here counting as separate poems the final six poems

which precede *Ripostes* in *Personae*: they are sections from a single long poem, "Und Drang," which concluded *Canzoni* (1911). Nor am I counting the Heine versions separately, as I do later in this chapter when thematic considerations are at issue. The five early volumes are reprinted, with the addition of other early poems from various sources, in *Collected Early Poems of Ezra Pound*, ed. Michael John King (New York: New Directions, 1976).

8. Richard Perceval Graves, *A. E. Housman: The Scholar-Poet* (New York: Scribner's, 1980), 171–72.

9. Quoted from Homberger, *Ezra Pound*, 287. Chesterton's review was published in 1934. Note two further illustrations: (1) Pound challenged a *Times* reviewer to a duel, because said reviewer thought too highly of Milton [Michael Alexander, *The Poetic Achievement of Ezra Pound* (Berkeley: University of California Press, 1979), 46]; (2) Pound declaimed a poem so loudly in a London restaurant that the management felt obliged to put a screen around his table [Patricia Hutchins, *Ezra Pound's Kensington: An Exploration, 1885-1913* (London: Faber and Faber, 1965), 129].

10. "The more anachronistic Pound becomes in his details, the more clearly does Audiart emerge as a pre-Raphaelite beauty," K. K. Ruthven, *A Guide to Ezra Pound's* Personae *(1926)* (Berkeley: University of California Press, 1969), 177.

11. Heymann, *Ezra Pound*, 15.

12. Pound, *Literary Essays*, 4–5.

13. Ibid., 9, 10–11.

14. Even so keen a critic as Ruthven is taken in: see *Guide*, 198–99.

15. H.D., *End of Torment*, 68.

16. Mary de Rachewiltz, *Discretions* (Boston: Little, Brown, 1971), reprinted by New Directions as a paperback entitled *Ezra Pound, Father and Teacher: Discretions*, n.d.

17. Stock, *Life of Ezra Pound*, 243.

18. Heymann, *Ezra Pound*, 56.

19. Sullivan, *Ezra Pound*, 33, 27.

20. William Chace, quoted from Donald Davie, *Ezra Pound* (New York: Viking, 1976), 118.

21. Levy, *Ezra Pound*, 3.

22. Heymann, *Ezra Pound*, 297.

23. Ibid., 75.

CHAPTER 3

1. Pound, *Gaudier-Brzeska*, 85, 44, 85.

2. Ibid., 88.

3. The next year, 1913, he wrote a good deal about contemporary French poetry: see Stock, *Life of Ezra Pound*, 137.

4. Ruthven, *Guide*, 41–42, 197–98.

5. "A Pact" was not collected until it appeared in *Lustra* (1916); it appeared in *Poetry* in 1913.

6. Pound, *Selected Prose*, 145–46.

7. Ezra Pound, *The Spirit of Romance* (London: Dent, 1910; reprint, New York: New Directions, 1968), 168.

8. Pound, *Letters*, 21.

9. *The Seafarer*, ed. I. L. Gordon (London: Methuen, 1960), 12. So too Stanley B. Greenfield's *A Critical History of Old English Literature* (New York: New York University Press, 1965), 220: "The persona of *The Seafarer* develops in outlook as the poem progresses: . . . when he thinks about the joys of God, all doubts and hesitations vanish, for in the mirror of eternity he recognizes the mutability of all earthly happiness." See, finally, the acute and detailed discussion in Neil D. Isaacs, *Structural Principles in Old English Poetry* (Knoxville: University of Tennessee Press, 1968), 35–55. Since Isaacs mentions my own work with Old English poetry, let me note that I have myself translated "The Seafarer," in Burton Raffel, *Poems From the Old English*, 2nd ed. (Lincoln: University of Nebraska Press, 1964), 31–34.

10. Ruthven, *Guide*, 62.

11. Pound, *Literary Essays*, 12.

12. Ibid., 3, 6, 9.

13. Ibid., 42.

14. Ibid., 43–45.

15. Ibid., 296.

16. Pound, *Letters*, 40.

17. Wai-lim Yip, *Ezra Pound's* Cathay (Princeton: Princeton University Press, 1969), 57.

18. Christine Froula, *A Guide to Ezra Pound's Selected Poems* (New York: New Directions, 1983), 45.

19. "Good art thrives in an atmosphere of parody," Pound wrote in 1913. "Parody is, I suppose, the best criticism." Pound, *Letters*, 13.

20. Pound, *Literary Essays*, 12.

21. Pound, *Letters*, 48–49.

22. Ibid., 69.

23. Ruthven, *Guide*, 44.

24. William Stanley Braithwaite, *Anthology of Magazine Verse for 1915* (New York: Laurence Gomme, 1915), 45, 229.

25. Davie, p. 36 and n. 5.

26. Ruthven, *Guide*, 190–91.

27. Pound, *Literary Essays*, 4, 11.

28. Quoted from Homberger, *Ezra Pound*, 335.

29. Pound, *Gaudier-Brzeska*, 126, 86.

30. Ibid., 86–87.

31. Ibid., 89.

32. Quoted from Froula, *Guide*, 61.

33. Pound, *Letters*, 179.

34. Ruthven, *Guide*, 160.
35. Alexander, *Poetic Achievement*, 73.
36. Pound, *Literary Essays*, p. 296 and n. 2.
37. Ibid., 297, 298, 299, 311.
38. Ibid., 294.
39. See Ruthven, *Guide*, 171.
40. Pound, *Letters*, 148.
41. Ibid., 135, 121, 239.
42. Lindberg-Seyersted, *Pound/Ford*, 33.
43. *The Autobiography of William Carlos Williams* (New York: New Directions, 1951), 58.
44. Quoted from Homberger, *Ezra Pound*, 205.
45. Pound, *Letters*, 248.
46. Ibid., 256.
47. Ibid., 113.
48. Pound, *ABC of Reading*, 13–14.
49. Pound, *Letters*, 243–44.
50. Ibid., 172.
51. Froula, *Guide*, 79.
52. For detailed information on background and influences the reader should consult John Espey, *Ezra Pound's* Mauberley (Berkeley: University of California Press, 1955; reprint, 1974).
53. "He has never been a pitiful figure. He has fought his fights with a very gay grimness and his wounds heal quickly." Ernest Hemingway, "Homage to Ezra" (1925), quoted from Russell, *Ezra Pound*, 75–76.
54. Pound, *Spirit of Romance*, 132.
55. *The Cantos of Ezra Pound* (New York: New Directions, 1970), 487.
56. Pound, *Letters*, 233.
57. Ibid., 128.
58. Froula, *Guide*, 97.
59. Ibid., 98.
60. Pound, *Letters*, 13.
61. Quoted from Ellen Williams, *Harriet Monroe and the Poetry Renaissance* (Urbana: University of Illinois Press, 1977), 95, 206.

CHAPTER 4

1. Pound, *Spirit of Romance*, 5, 7, 6.
2. Ibid., 6.
3. Ibid., 105–6.
4. Ibid., 145, 154.
5. Ibid., 201.
6. Quoted from Heymann, *Ezra Pound*, 10.

7. Pound, *Literary Essays,* 271.

8. Ibid., 268.

9. Pound, *Selected Prose,* 23.

10. Lindberg-Seyersted, *Pound/Ford,* 132.

11. Donald Carne-Ross, "Translation: Some Myths for its Making," *Delos* #1 (1968), 208–9.

12. Kenneth Quinn, *The Catullan Revolution* (Melbourne, Australia: Melbourne University Press, 1959; reprint, Ann Arbor: University of Michigan Press, 1971), 59–60.

13. *Catullus,* trans. Celia and Louis Zukofsky (New York: Grossman, 1969), unpaginated. For a fuller statement of this translation's inadequacies, see Burton Raffel, "No Tidbit Love You Outdoors Far As A Bier: Zukofsky's Catullus," *Arion* 8 (Autumn 1969): 435–45.

14. Pound, *Literary Essays,* 232, 238, 239. The essay was first published in 1917.

15. Pound, *ABC of Reading,* 48.

16. Pound, *Letters,* 82.

17. William Arrowsmith and Roger Shattuck, eds., *The Craft and Context of Translation,* rev. ed. (Austin: University of Texas Press, 1961; rev. ed., New York: Anchor Books, 1964), xxi.

18. Carne-Ross, "Translation," 208.

19. Hugh Gordon Porteus, "Ezra Pound and is Chinese Character," in Russell, *Ezra Pound,* 204.

20. Quoted from Sullivan, *Ezra Pound,* 105. Yip is critical of Eliot's comment but says himself that "the *vers libre* in *Cathay* prepared the language for later translators." Yip, *Cathay,* 163.

21. Yip, *Cathay,* 3. See also p. 82 and n. 15, and Stock, *Life of Ezra Pound,* 346.

22. Yip, *Cathay,* 181. The translation appears on pp. 192 and 194.

23. Ibid., 141–42.

24. Professor Donald Keene once remarked, in private conversation, that despite any and all errors, Pound's version of this poem was without a doubt the greatest ever produced in English.

25. Yip, *Cathay,* 148.

26. "Without personal involvement . . . the translator of poetry is almost certain to betray his author . . . [but] there is much more than mere personality involved in translation decisions. . . . The translator must work to the limits of his own taste." Burton Raffel, *The Forked Tongue: A Study of the Translation Process* (The Hague: Mouton, 1971), 22.

27. Yip, *Cathay,* 92–93, 84. "Even when he is given only the barest details, he is able to get into the central consciousness of the original by what we may perhaps call a kind of clairvoyance," ibid., 88.

28. *Ezra Pound: Translations* (New York: New Directions, 1954; enlarged ed., 1963), 436.

29. Pound, *Selected Prose,* 39.

30. Hugh Kenner, *The Poetry of Ezra Pound* (Norfolk, Conn.: New Directions, n.d. [1951]), 37.

31. Hugh Kenner, "The Muse in Tatters," *Arion* 7 (Summer 1968), 226.

32. Ruthven, *Guide*, 6, 7.

33. Stock, *Life of Ezra Pound*, 253.

34. Ibid., 274, quoting from a letter from W. B. Yeats to Lady Gregory.

35. Ibid., 246–47.

36. Ibid., 287.

37. Ibid., 321.

38. Sullivan, *Ezra Pound*, 23, 11.

CHAPTER 5

1. Pound, *Literary Essays*.

2. Ezra Pound, *Guide to Kulchur* (Norfolk, Conn.: New Directions, n.d. [1938]).

3. Stock, *Life of Ezra Pound*, 450.

4. Lindberg-Seyersted, *Pound/Ford*, 21.

5. Pound, *Letters*, 116–17.

6. Homberger, *Ezra Pound*, 287.

7. Pound, *Letters*, 296.

8. Pound, *Spirit of Romance*, 118.

9. Ibid., 156–57.

10. Ibid., 136.

11. Ibid., 216.

12. Ibid., 110.

13. Pound, *Selected Prose*, 366–68.

14. Ibid., 378–80.

15. Pound, *Literary Essays*, 91. As Pound wrote to Ford Madox Ford in 1922, "Am not really interested in anything that hasn't been there all the time." Lindberg-Seyersted, *Pound/Ford*, 66.

16. T. S. Eliot, "Tradition and the Individual Talent," *Selected Essays* (New York: Harcourt, Brace, 1950), 4.

17. T. S. Eliot, "To Criticize and Critic," *To Criticize the Critic* (London: Faber and Faber, 1965), 25.

18. T. S. Eliot, "The Frontiers of Criticism," *On Poetry and Poets* (New York: Noonday, 1961), 117.

19. Pound, *Literary Essays*, 92.

20. Pound, *Selected Prose*, 384.

21. Pound, *Literary Essays*, 216, 217.

22. Ibid., 218, 217, 216.

23. Pound, *Spirit of Romance*, 5.

24. Ibid., 126.

25. Ibid., 149, 163.

26. Ibid., 163.

27. Pound, *Literary Essays*, 215.

28. Pound, *Translations*, 24–25.
29. Pound, *Literary Essays*, 11.
30. Ibid., 5.
31. Ibid., 93.
32. Ibid., 94.
33. Ibid., 109, 111.
34. Ibid., 114.
35. Ibid., 115.
36. Ibid., 162, 168.
37. Ibid., 194.
38. Ibid., 199.
39. Pound, *Gaudier-Brzeska*, 119.
40. Quoted from Homberger, *Ezra Pound*, 466–67.
41. Pound, *Literary Essays*, xiii–xiv.
42. Stock, *Life of Ezra Pound*, 336.
43. Pound, *Guide to Kulchur*, 27.
44. Ibid., 289.
45. Ibid., 155–56.
46. Ibid., 177.
47. It is perhaps some support for mentioning *Guide to Kulchur* here, rather than in the concluding section of this chapter, that the book is ignored in Earle Davis, *Vision Fugitive: Ezra Pound and Economics* (Lawrence: University Press of Kansas, 1968).
48. Pound, *Letters*, 244. Eliot reprinted *How to Read* as the second essay in the section of *Literary Essays* entitled "The Art of Poetry."
49. Pound, *Letters*, 239.
50. Ezra Pound, *How to Read* (London: Desmond Harmsworth, 1931; reprint, New York: New Directions, n.d.), 8.
51. Ibid., 12–13.
52. Ibid., 16–17.
53. Pound, *Spirit of Romance*, 57.
54. Pound, *How to Read*, 18–19.
55. Suzanne K. Langer, *Philosophical Sketches* (Baltimore, Maryland: Johns Hopkins Press, 1962; reprint, New York: New American Library, 1964), 75–84. Langer is a leading writer on the philosophy of art; in my own view she is *the* leading writer.
56. Ibid., passim.
57. Pound, *How to Read*, 21.
58. *Melopoeia*, musically charged poetic language; *phanopoeia*, visually oriented poetic language; and *logopoeia*, culturally conditioned, ideational and emotional both, and essentially incapable of translation from one language to another, ibid., 25–26.
59. In this connection it is helpful to read Pound's essay, "Henry James," in *Literary Essays*, 295–338.
60. Pound, *ABC of Reading*, 89.
61. Ibid., 11.

62. Eric Roll, *A History of Economic Thought*, 3rd ed. (Englewood Cliffs, N.J.: Prentice-Hall, 1956), 457.

63. Pound, *Letters*, 138.

64. Ibid., 151.

65. Ibid., 158.

66. Ibid., 168.

67. Stock, *Life of Ezra Pound*, 221.

68. Quoted from ibid., 230–31.

69. Ibid., 313–14.

70. Pound, *Letters*, 204–5.

71. Stock, *Life of Ezra Pound*, 266.

72. Ibid., 278.

73. Ibid., 307.

74. Pound, *Letters*, 247. I have silently corrected what I take to be a clear typographical error which makes Pound say "It is a complex and as simple . . . "

75. Ibid., 341.

76. Ibid., 347.

77. Quoted from Stock, *Life of Ezra Pound*, 387.

78. Pound, *"Ezra Pound Speaking,"* 3–4.

79. Ibid., 7.

80. Ibid., 17–19.

81. Ibid., 20–22.

82. Ibid., 25–26.

83. Ibid., 28–30.

CHAPTER 6

1. *The Cantos of Ezra Pound* (New York: New Directions, 1970).

2. Quoted from Stock, *Life of Ezra Pound*, 28.

3. Ibid., 268–69.

4. Ibid., 289.

5. Russell, *Ezra Pound*, 67.

6. Ibid., 146, 137.

7. Ibid., 33.

8. George Dekker, *The Cantos of Ezra Pound* (New York: Barnes and Noble, 1963), 135, 202, 137.

9. Quoted from Homberger, *Ezra Pound*, 206.

10. Ibid., 446.

11. Ibid., 217.

12. Stock, *Life of Ezra Pound*, 291.

13. Kenner, *Poetry of Ezra Pound*, 186, 260, 274.

14. W. D. Snodgrass, in Homberger, *Ezra Pound*, 461.

15. Richard Eberhart, ibid., 385.

16. Sordello was a thirteenth-century Provencal poet. Browning's

poem, though it has narrative elements, is far more concerned with the "development of a soul." It is generally conceded to be a rather muddled and difficult work.

17. Ronald Bush, *The Genesis of Ezra Pound's Cantos* (Princeton, N.J.: Princeton University Press, 1976), 83.

18. Pound, *Letters*, 110.

19. Quoted from Bush, *Pound's Cantos*, 5.

20. Pound, *Pavannes and Divagations*, 50.

21. Ibid., 3-4.

22. Pound, *Literary Essays*, 327.

23. Quoted in Henry James, *The American Scene*, ed. Leon Edel (Bloomington: Indiana University Press, 1968), xxiii.

24. Leon Edel, *Henry James, The Master: 1901-1916* (Philadelphia: Lippincott, 1972), 317.

25. Bush, *Pound's Cantos*, 228, 229.

26. Ibid., 156.

27. Collected as "Pavannes," in Pound, *Pavannes and Divagations*, 79-105.

28. Bush, *Pound's Cantos*, 163.

29. Pound, *Pavannes and Divagations*, 79, 82.

30. Ibid., 87, 96.

31. Ibid., 64, 63, 65.

32. Burton Raffel, *T. S. Eliot* (New York: Frederick Ungar, 1982), 54-71.

33. Bush, *Pound's Cantos*, 238-39.

34. Raffel, *Eliot*, 66.

35. Bush, *Pound's Cantos*, 210-11.

36. Ibid., 21.

37. Quoted from *Life of Ezra Pound*, 228.

38. Bush, *Pound's Cantos*, 22.

39. Stock, *Life of Ezra Pound*, 19.

40. Pound, *Pavannes and Divagations*, 85.

41. *Selected Cantos of Ezra Pound* (New York: New Direction, 1970). There is a foreword, signed by Pound and dated 20 October 1966, which says inter alia: "I have made these selections to indicate main elements in the *Cantos*."

42. Dekker, *Cantos*, xvi.

43. Hemingway, *Letters*, 383.

44. Quoted from Russell, *Ezra Pound*, 78. Of these Greek passages Alexander writers: "There is no more splendid testimony to Pound's resource [sic] as a translator." Alexander, *Poetic Achievement*, 142. Are the *Cantos* also testimony to Pound "as a translator"?

45. Pound, *Letters*, 157.

46. Ibid., 114.

47. Alexander, *Poetic Achievemet*, 143.

48. Ibid., 142.

49. Pound, *Letters*, 227; Stock, *Life of Ezra Pound*, 253.

50. Quoted from *A Casebook on Ezra Pound*, ed. William Van O'Connor and Edward Stone (New York: Crowell, 1959), 31.

51. Ibid., 46.

52. Ibid., 51.

53. Charles Norman, *The Case of Ezra Pound* (New York: Funk and Wagnalls, 1968), 83.

54. Alexander, *Poetic Achievement*, 225-26.

55. Ibid., 221.

CHAPTER 7

1. Weintraub, *London Yankees*, 308.

2. *Selected Letters of Robert Frost*, ed. Lawrance Thompson (New York: Holt, Rinehart and Winston, 1964), 85–86.

3. *Family Letters of Robert and Elinor Frost*, ed. Arnold Grade (Albany: State University of New York Press, 1972), 161, 204.

4. Allen Tate, *Essays of Four Decades* (Chicago: Swallow, 1968), 512, 365.

5. Quoted from F. R. Leavis, *New Bearings in English Poetry* (London: Chatto and Windus, 1932; reprint, Harmondsworth, England: Penguin Books, 1963), 111, 126n.

6. *Letters of Archibald MacLeish*, ed. R. H. Winnick (Boston: Houghton Mifflin, 1983), 187, 188, 191, 193.

7. *The Letters of Hart Crane*, ed. Brom Weber (Berkeley: University of California Press, 1965), 54. The next year he insists that "my affection for Laforgue is none the less genuine for being led to him through Pound and T. S. Eliot," ibid., 88. Later in 1922, referring to a friend who "has developed a 'high hand' in criticism," Crane comments that it is "as effective and compelling as Pound's. I am beginning to see little Caesarian laurels sprouting," ibid., 95–96.

8. *The Journals of Sylvia Plath*, ed. Frances McCullough (New York: Dial, 1982), 290.

9. Horace Gregory, *The House on Jefferson Street: A Cycle of Memories* (New York: Holt, Rinehart and Winston, 1971), 175.

10. *Letters of Hart Crane and His Family*, ed. Thomas S. W. Lewis (New York: Columbia University Press, 1974), 126–27.

11. K. L. Goodwin, *The Influence of Ezra Pound* (London: Oxford University Press, 1966), 51, 93–94.

12. Ibid., 94, 102.

13. Ibid., 103, 104.

14. Ibid., 103.

15. Ibid., 120, 142.

16. E. E. Cummings, *A Miscellany Revised*, ed. George J. Firmage (New York: October House, 1965), 27.

17. *Selected Letters of E. E. Cummings*, ed. F. W. Dupee and George Stade (New York: Harcourt, Brace and World, 1969), 79, 104, 129.

18. Louise Bogan, *A Poet's Alphabet* (New York: McGraw-Hill, 1970), 336.

19. John Berryman, *The Freedom of the Poet* (New York: Farrar, Straus and Giroux, 1976), 253.

20. *Allen Verbatim*, ed. Gordon Ball (New York: McGraw-Hill, 1974), 180.

21. Robert Creeley, *A Quick Graph*, ed. Donald Allen (San Francisco: Four Seasons, 1970), 96.

22. Denise Levertov, *The Poet in the World* (New York: New Directions, 1973), 251.

23. *Letters of Wallace Stevens*, ed. Holly Stevens (New York: Knopf, 1966), 813.

24. Allan Seager, *The Glass House: The Life of Theodore Roethke* (New York: McGraw-Hill, 1968), 228.

25. Donald Hall, *Marianne Moore* (New York: Pegasus, 1970), 117.

26. Eileen Simpson, *Poets in Their Youth* (New York: Random House, 1982), 168.

27. David Perkins, *A History of Modern Poetry: From the 1890s to the High Modernist Mode* (Cambridge, Mass.: Harvard University Press, 1976), 451–52.

28. John Gross, *The Rise and Fall of the Man of Letters: English Literary Life Since 1800* (London: Weidenfeld and Nicolson, 1969; reprint, Harmondsworth, England: Penguin Books, 1973), 180.

29. Harry Levin, *Refractions* (New York: Oxford University Press, 1966), 188–89.

30. Graham Hough, *Image and Experience: Reflections on a Literary Revolution* (London: Duckworth, 1960; reprint, Lincoln: University of Nebraska Press, n.d.), 75–76, 99, 27.

31. Philip Rahv, *Essays on Literature and Politics, 1932–1972*, ed. Arabel J. Porter and Andrew J. Dvosin (Boston: Houghton Mifflin, 1978), 268.

32. Leslie Fiedler, *What Was Literature?* (New York: Simon and Schuster, 1982), 91, 92–93.

33. Matthew Josephson, *Life Among the Surrealists* (New York: Holt, Rinehart and Winston, 1962), 61, 89, 364.

34. R. P. Blackmur, *Form and Value in Modern Poetry* (New York: Harcourt Brace, 1952; reprint, New York: Anchor, 1975), 118–20.

35. Richard Kostelanetz, *The Old Poetries and the New* (Ann Arbor: University of Michigan Press, 1981), 49–51.

36. Randall Jarrell, *The Third Book of Criticism* (New York: Farrar, Straus and Giroux, 1969), 304–5.

37. Edmund Wilson, *Letters on Literature and Politics, 1912-1972*, ed. Elena Wilson (New York: Farrar, Straus and Giroux, 1977), 228. Wilson also confessed in 1920 to an unconscious cribbing of a Pound line for a poem of his own, ibid., 194.

38. Frederick J. Hoffman, *The Twenties* (New York: Viking, 1955), 163–64.

39. Horace Gregory, *Amy Lowell* (New York: Nelson, 1958), 84–85. Gregory notes that Pound had a special antipathy for Sir Edmund Gosse: "to Ezra Pound he stood for all that defined mediocrity in British literature," ibid., 85. Gregory observes, too, that Amy Lowell should have been convinced by Pound's actions that he "remained untainted by vanity and personal advancement," ibid., 103.

40. W.R. Johnson, *The Idea of Lyric* (Berkeley: University of California Press, 1980), 193.

41. Hugh Kenner, *A Homemade World: The American Modernist Writers* (New York: Knopf, 1975; reprint, New York: Morrow, 1975), 12–13.

42. Mario Praz, *The Flaming Heart* (Garden City, N.Y.: Anchor, 1958), 349.

43. Hemingway, *Letters*, 696.

Select Bibliography

Only books are here listed, and only those books which seem to me of use to and importance for the general reader.

BIBLIOGRAPHIC

Donald C. Gallup, *A Bibliography of Ezra Pound* (London: Hart-Davis, 1963)

EZRA POUND'S POETRY

Collected Early Poems of Ezra Pound, ed. Michael John King (New York: New Directions, 1976)
Personae: The Collected Poems of Ezra Pound (New York: Liveright, 1926; reprint, New York: New Directions, n.d.)
Selected Poems of Ezra Pound (New York: New Directions, 1957)
The Cantos of Ezra Pound (New York: New Directions, 1970)
Selected Cantos of Ezra Pound (New York: New Directions, 1970)
Ezra Pound: Translations (New York: New Directions, 1954; enlarged ed. 1963)

EZRA POUND'S PROSE

ABC of Reading (New Haven, Conn.: Yale University Press, 1934; reprint, New York: New Directions, n.d.)
Gaudier-Brzeska: A Memoir (London, John Lane, 1916; Reprint, New York: New Directions, 1970)
Guide to Kulchur (Norfolk, Conn.: New Directions, n.d. [1938])
How to Read (London: Desmond Harmsworth, 1931; reprint, New York: New Directions, n.d.)

Literary Essays of Ezra Pound, ed. T. S. Eliot (London: Faber and Faber, 1954; reprint, New York: New Directions)

Pavannes and Divagations (New York: New Directions, 1958)

Selected Prose, 1909-1965, ed. William Cookson (New York: New Directions, 1973)

The Spirit of Romance (London: Dent, 1910; reprint, New York: New Directions, 1968)

The Letters of Ezra Pound, 1907-1941, ed. D. D. Paige (New York: Harcourt Brace, 1950)

"Ezra Pound Speaking": Radio Speeches of World War II, ed. Leonard W. Doob (Westport, Conn.: Greenwood Press, 1978)

BIOGRAPHY

Noel Stock, *The Life of Ezra Pound*, rev. ed. (New York: Pantheon, 1970; reprint, San Francisco: North Point Press, 1982)

H. D., *End to Torment: A Memoir of Ezra Pound*, ed. Norman Holmes Pearson and Michael King (New York: New Directions, 1979)

C. David Heymann, *Ezra Pound: The Last Rower* (New York: Viking, 1976)

Patricia Hutchins, *Ezra Pound's Kensington: An Exploration, 1885-1913* (London: Faber and Faber, 1965)

Charles Norman, *The Case of Ezra Pound* (New York: Funk and Wagnalls, 1968)

Pound/Ford, The Story of a Literary Friendship: The Correspondence between Ezra Pound and Ford Madox Ford and Their Writings About Each Other, ed. Brita Lindberg-Seyersted (New York: New Directions, 1982).

Mary de Rachewiltz, *Discretions* (Boston: Little, Brown, 1971; reprint, New York: New Directions, as *Ezra Pound, Father and Teacher: Discretions*, n.d.)

CRITICISM

Michael Alexander, *The Poetic Achivement of Ezra Pound* (Berkeley: University of California Press, 1979)

Ronnie Apter, *Digging for the Treasure: Translation After Pound* (New York: Peter Lang, 1984)

Ian F. A. Bell, *Critic as Scientist: The Modernist Poetics of Ezra Pound* (London: Methuen, 1981)

Ronald Bush, *The Genesis of Ezra Pound's Cantos* (Princeton, N.J.: Princeton University Press, 1976)

Donald Davie, *Ezra Pound* (New York: Viking, 1976)

George Dekker, *The Cantos of Ezra Pound* (New York: Barnes and Noble, 1963)

John Espey, *Ezra Pound's* Mauberley (Berkeley: University of California Press, 1955; reprint, 1974)

Christine Froula, *A Guide to Ezra Pound's Selected Poems* (New York: New Directions, 1983)

K. L. Goodwin, *The Influence of Ezra Pound* (London: Oxford University Press, 1966)

Ezra Pound: The London Years: 1908-1920, ed. Philip Grover (New York: AMS Press, 1978)

Ernest Hemingway, *Selected Letters, 1917-1961*, ed. Carlos Baker (New York: Scribner's, 1981)

Ezra Pound: The Critical Heritage, ed. Eric Homberger (London and Boston: Routledge and Kegan Paul, 1972)

Hugh Kenner, *The Poetry of Ezra Pound* (Norfolk, Conn.: New Directions, n.d. [1951])

Alan Levy, *Ezra Pound: The Voice of Silence* (Sag Harbor, N.Y.: Permanent Press, 1983)

Stuart Y. McDougal, *Ezra Pound and the Troubador Tradition* (Princeton, N.J.: Princeton University Press, 1972)

A Casebook on Ezra Pound, ed. William Van O'Connor and Edward Stone (New York: Crowell, 1959)

M. L. Rosenthal, *A Primer of Ezra Pound* (New York: Macmillan, 1960)

An examination of Ezra Pound: A Collection of Essays to be presented to Ezra Pound on his 65th birthday, ed. Peter Russell (London: Peter Nevill, 1950)

K. K. Ruthven, *A Guide to Ezra Pound's* Personae *(1926)* (Berkeley: University of California Press, 1969)

Ezra Pound: A Critical Anthology, ed. J. P. Sullivan (Harmondsworth, England: Penguin Books, 1970)

J. P. Sullivan, *Ezra Pound and Sextus Propertius* (Austin: University of Texas Press, 1964)

Ezra Pound: A Collection of Critical Essays, ed. Walter Sutton (Englewood Cliffs, N.J.: Prentice-Hall, 1963)

Stanley Weintraub, *The London Yankees: Portraits of American Writers and Artists in England, 1894-1914* (New York: Harcourt Brace Jovanovich, 1979)

Ellen Williams, *Harriet Monroe and the Poetry Renaissance* (Urbana: University of Illinois Press, 1977)

Wai-lim Yip, *Ezra Pound's* Cathay (Princeton: Princeton University Press, 1969)

A Concordance to Personae: The Shorter Poems of Ezra Pound, ed. Gary Lane (New York: Haskell House, 1972)

Index

n.b. Works by writers other than Pound are ascribed to their authors; Pound's works are listed without authorial ascription.

Raffel, Burton.
   Ezra Pound, the prime minister of
poetry / Burton Raffel. -- Hamden,
Conn. : Archon Books, 1984.
   xii, 170 p. ; 23 cm.

   1. Pound, Ezra, 1885-1972--Criticism
and interpretation.

-1190-910731   VEHAcc   84-20533 r85